SOCIAL ACTION STORIES

"The stories in Social Action Stories are compelling and practical. In each diverse chapter—from how to create culturally relevant classrooms to framing potent community messages for under-represented groups—I received a quick, immediately usable idea that I could apply to a variety of environments. If you love stories and know there's power in them, this book will help you unleash the art form's full potential to make our world a better place."

—**Sue O'Halloran,** O'Halloran Diversity Productions, Culture of Civility

"All of these stories are beautifully and clearly written. I was moved to tears on many occasions as I read the struggles of people I didn't know and empathized with their stories. There is something for everyone to relate to, but importantly, there is much to learn. The suggested exercises at the end of each story deepen the thought process and allow the reader to dive further into possibilities and inspiration. This book belongs everywhere, in classrooms, community centers, and workplaces. These vital and meaningful stories need to be shared, as they open our eyes to the lives around us every day and give voice to those who may have none. In one of the stories, the image of a dandelion seed searching for the light will forever be a source of hope for me."

—**Wendy Woolfson** is a professional storyteller and facilitator specializing in supporting families and professionals to work collaboratively in meeting the needs of vulnerable children and young people through storytelling and trauma-sensitive practice. She is the creator of the Out of Harm Toolkit, which supports understanding of self-harm.

"**Storytelling is a powerful vehicle for change.** Compelling stories elicit strong emotional and cognitive responses and can drive post-narrative action. This richly edited book offers educators, students, and community leaders diverse stories highlighting universal human struggles and triumphs. Stories that can bring us together during a time of increasing polarization and disconnection, shifting the narratives we tell ourselves about the world and our roles in it. True to the book's vision, guided activities for listening to and reflecting upon our own and others' stories propel the reader to envision— and then work toward—more just and peaceful communities."

> **—Elizabeth O. Crawford, Ph.D.,** Associate Professor of Elementary Education at the University of North Carolina Wilmington specializing in instructional design and global social studies education and co-author of a book for K-8 educators, *Worldwide Learning: A Teacher's Guide to Shaping a Just, Sustainable Future.*

"**There are some stories we all need to hear.** *Social Action Stories* is a collection of dynamic narratives about why we teach and how we can be empowered to bring our whole selves to teaching. In their own voices, teachers and community activists examine gender, race, and culture in so many meaningful ways that every educator and movement worker can find a version of themselves in these narratives. Use this book to learn how to make empowering education and community a possibility for everyone.

> **—Bryan A. Brown,** a former high school science teacher, is an associate professor of science education at Stanford University, where he and his team conduct mixed methodological work exploring relationships between student identity, classroom culture, and academic achievement. He is the author of *Science In the City: Culturally Relevant STEM Education,* which was awarded the 2021 Outstanding Book Award from the American Association of Colleges for Teacher Education.

"**An inspired collection from a cadre of storytelling change advocates** who speak to the inherent strength and superpower that story has to move people to act, inspire, and transform their communities. It is filled with vivid examples and activities you can use to create more of the future you desire."

> **—Michael Margolis,** CEO, Storied, and author of *Turn the Impossible Into the Inevitable*

"**This book is essential in creating a sense of understanding** by sharing multiple stories of those from different perspectives. Not only does it share the lived experiences of those whose stories are included, it also provides many opportunities for readers to reflect on those lived experiences at the end of each story by creating learning opportunities to assist in forming a better society."

—**Jamie Holifield,** US and Global History/Equity & Student Engagement, Nicolet High School, Glendale, WI

"**Stories are powerful because they reach head and heart together** and activate our hands. A great story makes you want to take action. It helps you understand a different perspective, stand in someone else's shoes, and feel what they feel. This book is an essential call for action in times that ask us to wake up and take steps to create a more generative future for everyone. The combination of a short framing paragraph, the story itself, and the following Social Action Story Activity invite us on a powerful journey together. This collection shows how stories can serve us all.

—**Mary Alice Arthur,** author of *365 ALIVE! Find your voice. Claim your story*

"**Few things capture our imaginations like a riveting story.** The stories in this collection do more than simply entertain or teach. They inspire us to take action. In a time when inequities and trauma are rampant in communities worldwide, the work in Social Action Stories offers visions of hope, lessons about justice, and anecdotes about being the change. Many educators who want to work for Anti-bias and Anti-racism are unsure how to begin. These stories make us want to sit up and listen, then get up and act! And they offer guideposts about how to start."

—**Dana Lomax,** bilingual educator activist, Teacher Specialist in Ventura Unified School District, and Lecturer at CSUCI. A mentor and member of the social justice organization, Educators Doing Justice

"**This anthology has been masterfully created** by weaving stories relatable to everyone and educational to all. Reading it, we are left with the desire to tell our story, to take a mindful moment to hear other stories, and to pause and connect with one another about our shared text. This anthology of diverse authors has the potential to mirror our experiences. Through the Social Action Activities at the end of each story, this book comes alive and creates storytellers of readers themselves. This book is an excellent resource for the classroom, university, and any group ready to tell their stories.

—**Amy Melik,** ELL Teacher and Coordinator for a school district near Milwaukee, Wisconsin, Equity Specialist for BlackBlack and Associates, and board member, Learning for Justice.

"**Traumatic, confusing, and hard-to-discuss situations** are often most effectively explored from a safer space using story metaphor, folktales of long ago, or recent stories of others facing similar situations. I have learned that much-needed connection occurs when people engage as storytellers and active listeners. Bravo for the large number and variety of oral storytelling applications and activities found in *Social Action Stories* that demonstrate the deep influence storytelling can bring to choices made in life."

—**Dinny Biggs,** Canada, teacher and consultant, Former Coordinator of Mentoring, The Pathways to Education Program, Regent Park Community Health Centre, Toronto, Canada Past President, Storytellers of Canada—*Conteurs du Canada.*

"**This book is meant to open up dialogue** within your organization, community, or family as you develop a deeper understanding to grow with empathy, inclusiveness, and fairness. The stories provide a heightened awareness of the consequences of our actions, a realization that you are not alone. The activities offer new ways to embed inclusion and equity into your spheres of influence. As Wendy Welch states, in her story Deep Dive, 'We've all been there, that place where you feel so overwhelmed you can't think, can't hear, can't swallow. Your throat forgets how to function and the stone in your stomach feels like it's going to rip through your guts and fall on the floor.'"

—**June Cupido,** story weaver, Creative Director, Truth and Illusion Workshop.

SOCIAL ACTION STORIES

Impact Tales for the School and Community

Activist storytellers, educators, and organizers help us learn
a better story of our future

Edited by
Kevin D. Cordi, Ph.D., Kirstin J. Milks, Ph.D.,
& Rebecca Van Tassell

Foreword by Valeria Brown

Parkhurst Brothers Publishers
MARION, MICHIGAN

www.parkhurstbrothers.com

Consumers may order Parkhurst Brothers books from their favorite online or bricks-and-mortar booksellers, expecting prompt delivery. Parkhurst Brothers books are distributed to the trade through the Chicago Distribution Center. Trade and library orders may be placed through Ingram Book Company, Baker & Taylor, Follett Library Resources and other book industry wholesalers. To order from Chicago Distribution Center, phone 1-800-621-2736 or fax to 800-621-8476. Copies of this and other Parkhurst Brothers Publishers titles are available to organizations and corporations for purchase in quantity by contacting Special Sales Department at our home office location, listed on our web site. Manuscript submission guidelines for this publishing company are available at our web site.

Printed in the United States of America

First Edition, January, 2023

Printing history: 2023 2024 2025 2026 ... ... 8 7 6 5 4 3 2 1

Library Cataloging Data
1.   Principal Editor—Kevin D. Cordi, Ph.D.
2.   Subject—Oral Storytelling, 21st Century USA Culture, Americana
3.   Subject—Social Action in stories
2023-trade paperback and e-book

ISBN: Trade Paperback   978162491-171-2
ISBN: e-book   978162491-172-9

Cover and interior design by   Linda D. Parkhurst, Ph.D.
Acquired for Parkhurst Brothers Publishers by   Ted Parkhurst
Proofread by   Richard Culbertson

012023

To the stories

that make the world a better place,

and to their courageous, powerful tellers,

including you.

ACKNOWLEDGEMENTS

This book could not have been written without the amazing people who helped select and edit this text with me. These people are dedicated to social change and they, too, believe a story can promote and create action. I am thankful for my friend and colleague in social justice advocacy, Valeria Brown, for her poignant, powerful, and passionate forward. I also feel incredible gratitude for the other members of our editorial team, Kirstin Milks and Rebecca Van Tassell, for their talented and heartfelt work in editing and selecting texts along with Val. Thanks to our preliminary reading selection team at Ohio Northern University: Taylor Hesse, Taylor Daniel, and Ethan Smith. And, finally, I am thankful for my new beginning in working on social advocacy through storytelling at Ohio University Lancaster. This would not be possible without Ted Parkhurst asking me to begin this work. Thank you, Ted, for all you do.

—Kevin

To all the kids and grownups who have told me and shown me, repeatedly, that stories are worth it: thank you. Becky and Linda, your voices, in particular, are a part of me now, and I'm forever thankful. I'm also grateful to our contributors and the ways their stories have already recalibrated me; to Kevin, Becky, and Val for all I've learned through helping to put together this book; and to Parkhurst Brothers for amplifying the work and learning within these pages. Frank, Nemora, and Therian: you are my best teachers of how to be in this world. I love you.

   —Kirstin

I am grateful to so many people for supporting me and drawing me into the work of editing this collection. Thanks to all the incredible teachers who have invited me into their work, trusted me with their stories, and let me learn alongside them as they shared their stories with the wider world. Thank you to my colleagues at the Knowles Teacher Initiative—in particular Kirstin, Linda, and the staff of Kaleidoscope—for being an incredible learning community. Thank you to Kevin for many thoughtful and passionate conversations about storytelling, writing, publishing, and editing. I am so glad to have had the experience of working with this team to produce a volume that works toward equity through both its product and its process. And to my family, Josh, Henry & Esther, who have been patient during the many hours I've spent with my fingers on my keyboard.

   —Rebecca

CONTENTS

FIGURES

INTRODUCTION
THE IMPACT WE CAN MAKE WITH STORY

Kevin Cordi

What does it mean to tell a social action story? And what does it mean to tell such a story now? When sharp words and policies are used to belittle people because of their gender, culture, race, place of birth, community, or income level, we can respond first by listening and not by telling.

"Go back to your country." "There are some very fine people on both sides." "We need a wall." Think how destructive these words and others are when uttered or screamed. Often, these loud words are the first to be heard.

However, merely because these voices are loud does not mean they are important. There is another story to be told.

———

I can't say I know what it is like to be anything firsthand but what I am, an Appalachian cisgender white male. I know my narrative as a first-generation poor college student who became a college professor teaching in rural and urban high schools and then in universities in California and Ohio. I can't speak from direct experience of the inequity experienced by LBGTQ+ people, African American people, Latinx people, and others whose stories are rooted in struggle. What I can speak to, and what we created this book to address, is the need for these stories to teach us and inspire us to action. Story can help people move from thinking about a difference to making a difference—a difference that works.

Story has the power to hear of lives and experiences yet untold, to deeply listen to stories of resistance, loss, pain, and inequity. Story can be a catalyst to help one see how privilege often filters, censors, and hides a life. It can tell why wearing a particular style of red cap in America harms others—and, when people stop to listen to why it causes distress, they can help others consider not wearing it.

If we only hear the hate, the rhetoric of division, from our news sources and social media feeds, how can we come together and advocate change?

We need to tell and hear the stories that lead us to wonder, question, inquire, and act.

For the last 25 years, I have listened, studied, and practiced the art of compassionate storytelling. As Parker Palmer says in *The Courage to Teach* (2017),

> We cannot see what is 'out there' merely by looking around. Everything depends on the lenses through which we view the world. By putting on new lenses, we can see things that would otherwise remain invisible.

Reading, listening, and telling action stories renders people and their stories visible. This book chronicles voices from storyteller-activists, educational reformers, and community organizers, voices whose stories serve as an optometrist's kit of drops and lenses to assist us as we experience our world in new ways. It's filled with testimony and narratives from ordinary people working for change. We hope you find solace, inspiration, and companionship in their words.

This book also serves as a useful guide. Along with each story, we've included one or more activities—developed by the contributors and the editorial team—to help increase your capacity as a learner, storyteller, and activist. Some activities derive from personal reflections, but many come out of work in community. Story is connected to a vast array of detailed actions that have moved people to consider their thinking. Some of these actions are quiet, while others may be complex and intense. We hope working through some or all of the activities will help you imagine and redefine your own array of reactions and responses.

Let us listen deeply, share these tales, and resist the ugly, uninformed accounts that creep our schools, communities, and homes.

Instead, tell your story, and listen to far more than you tell.

Some additional notes about this book:

• After reading the powerful accounts that flooded in after we made the call for submissions for this book—those that are included and those that were not—we discovered there are multitudes of rich and diverse stories that promote deliberate and significant action. There are multitudes of rich and diverse stories that promote deliberate and significant action. However, not all important stories and issues in our time are represented in this collection. Rather, the editorial team sees this volume as a sampler, showing how social action can be experienced at different times in a career or a lifetime. We trust this collection will make it clear that you are not alone.

• This collection does not avoid hard stories. They are not included for shock value, but rather to show why and how these stories matter. Such stories teach us the world is not the same for all, that we must actively seek to understand its complexity.

• We'd love to know how you're using this book in your journey as an educator, a storyteller, an activist, or some combination. We'd also love to know the types of issues you care about and whether or not you'd be interested in submitting a story to a potential next volume of social action stories. Please feel free to reach out!

As I write this, I've only now returned from hearing Parkland survivor and advocate Samantha Fuentes, who suffered from the endless onslaught of bullets at that high school on that terrible day. She told us her story could be one of hate because "it is easy to hate … but it takes more labor to love." In Samantha's words, "Everyone can tell stories, but it is the impact that makes it a great story."

We editors—Kirstin, Rebecca and Kevin—hope that, wherever you are in your journey, you find solace, inspiration, courage, and pathways to your action—*your* impact—through the contents of this collection.

Together, we can make a difference with stories.

FOREWORD

Val Brown

I COULDN'T EXPLAIN MY TEARS. However, as I dropped my oldest child—one of my two greatest inspirations—off on his first day of middle school, the tears would not stop rolling down my face. I thought all I would feel was giddy, bubbly, and confident that I had prepared him to go out into the world. But I didn't. I felt nervous, melancholy, and worried. Had I had done enough?

"I am an expert in double-digit ages and middle school years," I had told him since he turned eleven, reassuring him that he would be well-equipped for this next stage in life. As a middle school graduate and former middle school teacher, I could teach him everything he needed to know to survive the next three years. I knew he would form incredible lifelong friendships. I knew he would be challenged academically. And I knew there was nothing to worry about. The first day of middle school is a happy day. Right?

Yet I could not explain my tears.

The last time I remember feeling so moved by a school experience with him was the summer before he entered kindergarten. We lived just one block away from his future school and would pass the building every time we left our home.

"Look, there is your new school where you will be attending kindergarten," I said to him one day as we were driving by. "It is going to be awesome."

"Will I have a brown teacher?" asked my then-five-year-old.

He was in his booster seat behind my driver's seat, and he could not see my face, which was a mix of shock and sadness at his loss of innocence. This was the first time I remember my son ever explicitly asking a question about racial identity. It was undoubtedly the first time that he ever had a question about the racial identity of his teachers. I had not considered that he had spent any time thinking about it, even though I had.

In the moments before I answered him, many different ideas ran through my mind.

First, I went back to the moment our gynecologist told us the assigned sex of our child.

"It's a boy," she said excitedly.

My husband was visibly thrilled, and I smiled. Underneath my smile, though, was a rising wave of anxiety. My husband and I are Black, which means, without a doubt, we would give birth to a Black child. At the moment that she announced we were having a boy, I felt the entire weight of those words on my shoulders. Black boys remain more likely to be suspended and expelled, less likely to be enrolled in accelerated courses, and consistently lag behind all other racial groups when it comes to achievement on standardized tests (de Brey et al., 2018). Statistically speaking, it would not be surprising if he did not find joy and support in school.

On top of that, it was the summer of 2013. As a family and a community, we were all still reeling from the murder of Trayvon Martin. In February 2012, Trayvon was shot and killed in a neighborhood across the street from one of our elementary schools. Trayvon's death launched a national response from racial justice and civil rights activists and the creation of #BlackLivesMatter. Even still, I could not guarantee my son's safety outside the comforts of our home.

Finally, my husband and I were both Black educators. There are not that many of us; the percentage of Black educators in public elementary and secondary schools is 7 percent (de Brey et al., 2018). My husband and I both worked in the district. I knew that if all things remained the same—and our son went to the elementary, middle, and high schools in the feeder pattern—he would have only a few opportunities to have Black teachers before graduating. In middle school, I would be the choice. In high school, it would be his father.

I looked in my rearview mirror. My son was waiting patiently for an answer. I am not sure how much time passed before I answered him, but when I finally spoke up, my words followed a deep sigh.

"No, son, but I know your teachers will be very nice," I said with a reassuring smile.

———

This exchange with my almost-kindergartner, which lasted no more than two minutes, reminded me I had work to do. As an educator and the reigning district teacher of the year, I felt it was my opportunity to advocate for more teachers of color in our district. I honestly thought a simple email would do the trick. It went something like this:

> *Dear [Superintendent]:*
> *Teachers of color are really important for all students. Let me*
> *know if I can help you recruit some at upcoming job fairs.*
> *Sincerely,*
> *Val*

I hit send, patted myself on the back, and congratulated myself on a job well done. "Go, Val, go!" I said to myself.

The superintendent responded, "Great," and I thought I had inserted myself as a helper into a well-oiled machine of recruiting diverse teacher candidates. I learned a few weeks later that there was undoubtedly no machine. I had so much to learn.

Over that school year and the three that followed, several pieces of my own social action to recruit and retain teachers of color started to come together.

Win: The superintendent introduced me to two Black male assistant principals who had separately advocated for increased representation among the teachers of color. We began meeting informally and remarked that, although we had all worked in the district for many years, we never had the opportunity to meet one another.

Reality check: In fact, we noted that unless teachers of color worked at the same school, there was no opportunity to be in community with one another. Immediately after our first meeting, we knew that not only was recruiting teachers of color vital, we also needed to retain the ones we had by helping them form a sense of community.

Win: I was able to attend the local college job fairs to help recruit teachers of color.

Reality check: Unfortunately, there were few—if any—teacher of color candidates to recruit. I learned very quickly that students of color were not choosing majors in colleges of education. They were nowhere to be found, *except* at historically Black colleges and universities (HBCUs). Even then, candidates did not necessarily want to relocate to my city.

Win: I got approval to host a reception for teachers of color.

Reality check: While I got approval, I did not get a budget. Any money we needed to support our mission had to be raised by the group. Also, everyone I recruited to be on the team, like myself, had full-time jobs as teachers, assistant principals, and district personnel.

———

For several reasons, my husband and I left the district in 2016. That didn't fare well for retention numbers, and I am not sure if teachers of color were actively recruited to replace us. That saddens me. Plus, I am super self-critical; the result is that I honestly cannot say if my efforts led to increasing recruitment or retention.

I can say, though, that our team tried. As I mentioned, there was no well-oiled machine in which we could insert ourselves and easily contribute. There were only a few cogs, springs, and a hammer. We worked as hard as we could to make something with every tool we had at our disposal.

I can say that we educated the administrators and hiring personnel in our district. We became the practitioners and leaders other people turned to when they had questions about diversity and inclusion.

I can say that we connected educators of color to one another. We helped them feel seen and honored for the contributions they made to our district and its students.

I can also say that the experience led me to a few reflection questions I keep in my heart when embarking on any new social action endeavor:

How will I serve the people?
How can my learning inform my strategy?
How will I make sure I have the resources I need?
How do I define short-term and long-term success?
How do I walk away when it is time?

Acting on my son's behalf changed everything for me. It opened up a passion in me that I did not know existed. Before taking these steps, I considered myself "just a teacher," but I learned that assistant principals, principals, superintendents, and school board members would listen to me. The experience drove me to connect with others outside of my district who were equally passionate about educators of color. I learned about the benefits and challenges of collective organizing. I bumped into the brick walls of resistance that support the status quo.

The work of social action is incredibly messy, and you should know that anyone who acts will be left with bumps and bruises. Movement, by definition, requires opening yourself up to risk. To complicate matters, you often take steps in the dark. Struggles are hard-fought and wins are hard-won. Loses can profoundly impact the lives of others. Most times, you are not sure if what you are doing will matter.

In *Social Action Stories,* you have the opportunity to hear stories from people of all walks of life. You'll learn what others did, why they did it, and how they did it; whether they experienced success, and if not, how they dealt with failure.

I believe that all of our actions matter, and so I have continued to act in ways that feel big and small. I challenge you to not only read this book for the stories of our successes and failures but also use it as a catalyst for your own actions. We need you, too. Your inspiration may come when you least expect it.

Fast forward seven years. I was the first in the pick-up line outside of the middle school. My son climbed in the car confidently, beaming ear-to-ear and relishing the newfound freedom of switching classes. He showed me that he was going to be alright, and I could tuck away my worries for another day. I was grateful.

═══

Reference

de Brey, C., Musu, L., McFarland, J., Wilkinson-Flicker, S., Diliberti, M., Zhang, A., Branstetter, C., and Wang, X. (2019). *Status and Trends in the Education of Racial and Ethnic Groups 2018* (NCES 2019-038). U.S. Department of Education. Washington, DC: National Center for Education Statistics. Retrieved from https://nces.ed.gov/pubsearch/.

VAL BROWN is a professional development facilitator for a national non-profit whose role primarily includes designing, facilitating, and evaluating anti-bias professional development for educators across the country. For 14 years prior to joining her current organization, Val worked in public K-12 education and higher education as a teacher, instructional coach, district administrator, and professional learning specialist. She is also the founder of #ClearTheAir, a body of educators who believe that community, learning, and dialogue are essential to personal and professional growth—as well as a wife and mother.

Social Action Story Activity for the Introduction
Quick Write

One of the most powerful tools we have to grow our capacity as activists is the power of reflection. By writing out our stories in a private space, we can discover our passions, find direction, and renew our commitment to a better future.

Below are the five questions Val lists as her guideposts when working on a social action endeavor. Find a quiet time to write or type, set a timer for seven minutes, and select one or more of the following questions as you reflect on one of your current projects or ideas.

- *How will I serve the people?*

- *How can my learning inform my strategy?*

- *How will I make sure I have the resources I need?*

- *How do I define short-term and long-term success?*

- *How do I walk away when it is time?*

If you already have collaborators in the work you're writing about, do this quick-write independently, then share your ideas and reflections.

You might also set a reminder on your calendar to check in with the results of your quick write in a month, six months, or a year to ask:

- *What's changed?*

- *What's stayed the same?*

- *Is one of these questions now more pressing than it was?*

- *What have you learned about yourself or your work?*

We'll revisit many of Val's questions throughout the book!

TIME: ACTING FOR PRESENT AND FUTURE CHANGE

WE CAN'T ALWAYS SEE OR KNOW THE IMPACT OF OUR ACTIONS on those around us. In fact, those we impact might not recognize it right away. As we see in the stories in this section, our daily interactions with others may produce an "ah-ha" moment or may leave us feeling troubled or unsuccessful. We might not see the impact of our actions on a patient until 20 years later, and we might still be in the middle of the incremental work of building relationships. We could have unanticipated experiences with others that affirm our work and provide us hope. To act for present and future change, we must update our concept of time. The stories that follow can show us how reflection can be a powerful tool to do so.

DANDELION

MICHAEL WILLIAMS

There is action in listening, deep listening. Sometimes, we may
be present, but we are not listening. Michael reminds us of the value of
listening as an active process—and that we might not know just how large
an impact our listening may have.

SHE WAS A WEED OF A GIRL—TOUGH, SPINDLY AND SPIKY. Yet there was
something fragile about her too—the downcast eyes, waif-like expression,
and the alarming gauntness of her body. Her short-cropped red hair and
featureless body made it difficult to tell whether she was a young girl or
boy.

Diana (not her real name) was the newest resident to be put on my
caseload. I was a childcare worker, fresh from college, and now the only
male counselor at a residential treatment center for adolescent women.
My job was to meet regularly with the young women, offer counseling,
and encourage their well-being. Most of them had experienced abuse of
one sort or another.

Diana had suffered terribly for most of her fourteen years—verbal,
emotional, physical, and sexual abuse at the hands of her father. In recent

years, she had tried starving herself, becoming severely anorexic, and following a recent suicide attempt, she had been hospitalized. Although still considered a suicide risk, she was placed in our care with the hope that she might recover in our residential program.

For weeks, our counseling sessions were mostly silent affairs. I'd ask questions and invite her to engage in some light conversation, but mostly we'd sit in silence, Diana mute and scrunched up at the end of the sofa with a blanket wrapped tightly around her. The most I could hope for was that I might provide a safe enough space for her to relax and open up.

I would wait a long time, but one day, something happened. Out of the silence, Diana began to speak quietly and without making eye contact. She began to tell me her story. Now I was the silent one.

I was afraid to speak for fear of interrupting the flow of Diana's story. Although initially hesitant and broken, her voice gained strength, her words spilling into the room. I felt speechless in the wake of the details of her story. Although I'd read accounts of abuse and heard some of the girls share bits of their stories in our weekly group therapy sessions, nothing could prepare me for Diana's nightmare. I sat there on the verge of tears, feeling sick, angry, helpless, and ashamed for what a man—a father— could do to his daughter.

Suddenly, I was aware that our hour together was coming to a close. Diana had exhausted herself and retreated into her shell once again, pulling the blanket even more tightly around her. I felt compelled to offer her something, some soothing advice. After all, I thought, I was the coun-selor. But I couldn't think of anything that would begin to help. Nothing in my counseling textbooks or training seemed relevant. Then out of nowhere, an image came to mind—the image of a dandelion.

I told Diana of a little seed deep down in the dark earth and how it began to wriggle about in the darkness. All it knew was that it had to find the light. Down went its roots, searching for moisture. Up went its head, searching for a sustainable space and the slightest hint of light. But rocks and hard earth blocked its way. Turning this way and that, it kept searching, finding a drop of moisture here, a small crevice there. The dandelion (for that was what it was) struggled upward.

Then, just when it thought it might succeed, the dandelion sprout bumped its head on the hard underside of the concrete that men had laid on the earth above. There didn't seem to be any hope of finding the light. Yet Dandelion didn't give up. She kept moving, twisting and turning, finding a little space to grow and push.

Finally, after a great deal of effort, she broke through the hard pavement, broke through into the morning light. She breathed fresh air and, for the first time, stretched her body upward, turned her face to the golden sun, and basked in its warmth. For the first time, she felt free.

That was the end of my story. Our time was up. Diana rose from the sofa without any comment and left the room.

I eventually left the center to return to university and take up an academic career, which eventually took me overseas. Diana remained at the center and continued with her recovery.

Twenty years passed. Memories faded.

One day, while on a return visit to my hometown and family, I was out shopping. Just as I was leaving the store, a voice called my name. I turned to see a radiant, red-haired woman smiling and waving at me. I didn't recognize her. She approached and introduced herself. It was Diana. Now in her thirties, she radiated confidence, appearing to be the very model of a joyful woman. We exchanged details of our lives. She had finished school, gone to university, gotten a degree in social work, and was now the local women's shelter director. I was amazed at the transformation and incredibly proud of her.

As we prepared to part, she became silent for a moment, then looked up at me with soulful eyes. "Michael," she began, "do you remember the story you told me?"

Nothing came to mind. "I'm sorry," I smiled, "I think I told a lot of stories in those days. I was known for being a bit of a storyteller."

"Well," she laughed, "you told me a story about a dandelion, and I've never forgotten it. In fact, I thought about it a lot back then. It really helped me."

It all came flooding back. The dandelion. The story had come from nowhere in a moment of desperation.

"I don't know where that story came from," I admitted, "I just sort of made it up. I didn't know what else to do or say to you."

Diana explained to me how important the story had become to her and confessed, laughingly, that she had used the story many times with her own clients.

"I guess the story found us just at the right time," I said.

Then, Diana paused again and said, "There's another thing too … that day we met … when I told you my story … that was the first time anyone had listened to the *entire* story from beginning to end without stopping me or trying to fix me or telling me that everything was going to be okay."

Diana went on to explain how when she had tried to tell her mother about the abuse, she had interrupted and told Diana not to tell anyone for fear of bringing shame on the family, then went on giving her false promises that the abuse would stop. At school, Diana had summoned up the courage to tell a teacher, but the teacher too interrupted, advising her to tell her mother. And later, when she went into care, her story had been interrupted by the social worker who tried to reassure Diana that everything would be okay. No one had allowed Diana to tell her story. "You were the first person," she said, "who simply sat and listened to the story from beginning to end."

Diana taught me three very important things that day. First, I learned there is no greater agony than bearing an untold story (as the poet Maya Angelou has so succinctly put it). Second, Diana demonstrated that a person's story needs to be heard from beginning to end without interruption, without the listener's need to give false hope, to fix, or to reassure. Finally, Diana taught me never to underestimate the power of a humble story, a story that comes when and where you least expect it. Often, I've since realized, that story emerges as if through concrete to blossom, has its moment in the light and warmth of the morning sun, and passes its indomitable spirit on to us.

———

Michael Williams is a professional storyteller, story coach, writer, and radio host who has worked internationally with individuals as well as community and corporate organizations for more than twenty years. His integration of counseling, teaching, and narrative practices helps clients become compassionate communicators, creative and innovative leaders, and practitioners able to gain a deeper understanding and appreciation of how story is essential to creating a better world for all.

Social Action Story Activity for "Dandelion"
Active Listening

To truly hear, we must practice the skills of listening. Listening is a conscious gift we give others.

Working with a partner, share a story of a time you overcame a difficulty or challenge. Consider questions like:

- *What was the situation before the difficulty?*

- *What was the nature of the difficulty?*

- *How did you meet or overcome the difficulty?*

- *What did you learn about yourself and others as a result?*

As a listener, practice listening without interruption. Check your impulse to over-empathize, "fix," or reassure your partner. The listener's task here is to provide a safe space for the story to emerge.

After both partners have had a chance to share their stories, take time to thank one another and reflect on the experience.

Moving forward, consider practicing listening more intentionally in conversation or meetings. Often, we are quick to provide an opinion or fix a problem, but if we want to promote social change, we need to hear and reflect on stories before we know how to tell them or use them together.

A RED HAT

Lyn Ford

Social action is about working against fear. Too often, our fear divides us. We even wear shirts, hats, and pins that advocate our views. But what happens when you have to ride in the car with someone who wears something that makes you feel afraid? In Lyn's story, we find out.

I HAD WAITED LONGER THAN EXPECTED for my transportation to a conference to arrive at the airport and take me to the location. I was tired, cold, and hungry when I saw the white minivan with the appropriate name on its side come around the pickup driveway and slow down.

Out stepped my driver. He was wearing a red hat.

In any other decade, that would have meant nothing more than he was wearing a red hat. But in this decade … and it had that statement on it, in white letters.[1] I was afraid, afraid of him, because of a red hat.

My apprehension must have shown in my face. He stopped and asked, "Are you waiting for a ride to the campus?"

"Yes," I said.

---

1   The white letters are "MAKE AMERICA GREAT AGAIN," often referred to as MAGA, a campaign slogan for U.S. President Donald Trump.

"Lyn Ford?" he asked.

"Yes," I said.

"Hmpf," he hmpfed. "For a storyteller, you're awfully quiet."

Okay, he knew I was going to a storytelling conference. He knew my name. He showed me his orders to pick up and transport one "Lyn Ford," and the confirmation number on the paper matched mine. I got into the back seat. He closed the door and put my bag in the back of the minivan. We headed to the campus, one hour from the airport.

One hour. I looked at the sticker on the dashboard, a red sticker with the names of two candidates, neither of whom had gotten my vote.

I thought it would be best not to speak. He didn't seem to have the same thought.

"So, you're a storyteller. What do you do?"

"I tell stories … " I said. Then, realizing that response might have sounded as though I thought he was ignorant, I added, "… and I tell stories to kids and adults in schools and libraries and other places, and I help people work on their writing and spoken-word presentations, and …"

"So, what are you doing at the university?" he interrupted.

"I'm encouraging teachers to use stories and storytelling skills as teaching tools for grades K through 2."

"And somebody's going to pay you for that?" he asked. I couldn't see his face. I'd sat behind him. I moved over so that I could see his eyes in the rearview mirror.

I laughed, "Sometimes people pay me. Yes."

He laughed. Then he said, "People are fools. Anybody can tell a story."

There were so many things I wanted to say. I stuck to the details of educating, informing, of passing on traditions—not just entertaining.

"What are your traditions?" He interrupted again. "What kind of traditions do you have? I mean, where'd your people come from? You know, there's so many foreigners around here …."

There it was, I thought, there was the beginning of a red hat analysis of my olive skin, my dark eyes, my wide nose, my curly hair.

I asked him, "Where'd *your* people come from?"

He said, "Oh, I'm from West Virginia, Appalachian born and bred."

I said, "I'm from Appalachia, too. Pennsylvania. We're *Affrilachian.* And some of my folks lived near Wheeling."

"Affrilachian???" Tell me about that," he said.

As I talked, his eyes seemed to crinkle at the edges. I hoped that meant he was smiling. When the van stopped for a traffic light, he turned to me, seemed to be looking for something he'd recognize in my eyes.

Slowly he turned around. The light changed to green. His voice deepened. "You ever use a gun?" he asked.

"No," I said, "but some in my family went hunting, for food, not for trophies."

"That's the way to do it," he said, and his eyes crinkled again.

The rest of the trip was a river of chatter about wild grapes and sour cherries and apples picked and eaten in their season, about the beauty in the change of seasons. About how we both missed the Appalachian hills and valleys, for this place was as flat as the area I now call home.

One hour was too short for our conversation.

When we got to the campus, he opened my door. He held out his hand to help me from my seat. I took his hand. He shook mine.

Before he got my bag, he said, "When you call for your ride back to the airport, you ask for me. Folks around here don't know much about the hills. I'd love to talk with you some more."

I promised I would.

When we arrived at the airport again four days later, he took my hand again. His handshake was warm, and so was his smile. "I hope you come back this way again, Miz Lyn," he said. It's good to talk to people who know the hills."

I thanked him for a pleasant ride. He watched me walk my roller bag into the airport. I waved again.

He tipped his red hat.

LYNETTE (LYN) FORD is an internationally recognized Affrilachian storyteller, teaching artist, and author, and a two-time recipient of the National Storytelling Network's ORACLE Circle of Excellence award.

Social Action Story Activity for "A Red Hat"
Going Against the Grain

We all know people that disagree with others' views, sometimes vehemently. However, this activity asks you to engage safely in a conversation that's not about an issue over which you and your dialogue partner disagree. Rather, your goal is to find the common stories and perspectives that you share.

Conversations about critical social issues are not safe for many people at many times. Consider where you are, geographically, temporally, physically, and emotionally, before deciding to engage in this activity.

Ask a person to serve as a dialogue partner, explaining that you want to find common ground and that, although you disagree on some major areas, you are open to listening and learning about each other.

When you can, seek out times to talk and exchange stories with people with whom you disagree. Perhaps you might find common ground for change.

LISTENING TO J.

Sherrill Knezel

Many teachers are in the middle of learning how to work towards racial justice in their classrooms. Sherrill struggled with how she, a White woman, could make a difference before realizing she didn't need to solve all racism. Instead, she started in her own circle of influence, building trust and relationship with one student.

J. CAME INTO THE ART ROOM FROM LUNCH with the rest of his fourth-grade class, talkative and unsettled. I could feel my stomach tense a bit, wanting to help him make a good transition to the start of class but not knowing quite what would work. I made eye contact and greeted him, asking how his day had been going. "OK," he said and ambled to his table. As the students settled in, I started class like I always do. "Who wants to read the quote or the icons?"

On the smart board, I display an inspirational quote along with six visual icons to remind students about expectations during class. A student at the back of the room raised her hand, and when I called on her, she read a quote widely attributed to Maya Angelou: "I've learned that people will forget what you said, people will forget what you did, but people will never forget how you made them feel."

"Does anyone know who Maya Angelou is?" I asked.

J. had been sitting with his back to the board. When he heard me ask the question, he whipped around and said with a bit of reverence in his voice, "She's a legend!" This made me smile: "I know!" I got excited telling J. that she was one of the top three people in the whole world with which I would have loved to meet and share a meal. That wish was one small thing we had in common … that was a start!

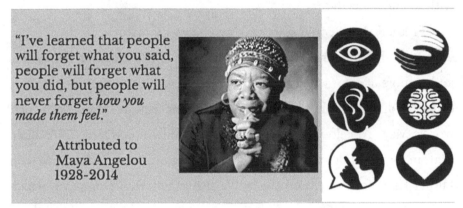

"I've learned that people will forget what you said, people will forget what you did, but people will never forget *how you made them feel.*"

Attributed to
Maya Angelou
1928-2014

Figure 1. Maya Angelou Quote/Class Expectations

A bit of background: J. had transferred to our school the year before, partway into 3rd grade. An athletic kid with a great smile and quick wit, J. also had a quick temper, and the transition of getting used to a new school and new classmates had been bumpy. I had struggled to make a connection with him.

I had grown since last year, though. I knew that building a relationship with J. and centering his lived experience, interests, and knowledge was the way to forge trust. Thanks to a Twitter chat group and PLN (Professional Learning Network) called #ClearTheAir, I had read books on social justice, race, Black history, White fragility, and White rage. I began learning from teachers of color and other White educators how to hold space, listen to, and empower students of color.

I also started constantly monitoring my Whiteness, privilege, and implicit biases in order to stay aware of their influence on how I inter-preted student behavior. Was I assuming that all of my students had the same frame of reference and life experience that I had as a White female educator? Was I misinterpreting behaviors of my students of color as negative when I would characterize those same behaviors as self-advocacy with White students?

I knew that I could start making change in my own circle of influ-ence, with the students in my art classroom, so I began seeking out leaders and authors of color when choosing opening quotes for my 3rd-5th grade classes. I displayed photos of these leaders and authors along with their words: Maya Angelou, Jesse Owens, James Baldwin, Madame CJ Walker, Marian Wright Edelman, Booker T. Washington, Jesse Jackson, Martin Luther King, Jr., and Alice Walker. We also practiced *sketchnoting*, which author Tammy McGregor describes as visual note-taking that makes thinking visible and meaningful. Using StoryCorps podcasts that centered the lived experience of people of color.

I honestly don't know if any of my White students noticed the change, but J. did. Each week when we read the quotes, he had insights to share. J was also more engaged when Black history came up—especially anything to do with slavery. J. shared that he had watched the movie *Roots*, and asked me if I knew what White people had done to Black people in the movie. I shared that I had seen it, that it was powerful and that I had found it hard to watch.

After this exchange, I started calling on J. more to read the quote or talk about what the icons meant to him that day. What I really began to see in J. was a leader and a passionate student who had potential to do great things when he applied himself.

A few weeks later, J. walked in after lunch seeming to need attention, joking around instead of getting to his table. I called on a student to read the quote and then asked if anyone wanted to do the icons. I called on one student to do the first column, "Eyes watching, ears listening, voices quiet when someone else is talking." The student finished. "Anyone want to do the second column?" I asked.

Usually students say, "Hands in your lap. Brains thinking. Hearts caring." We always talk about how the icons can mean different things to different people and may even mean different things on different days depending on what happened to you that day.

J. raised his hand. I hesitated—J. might take it seriously or he could take it off the rails. It would take time to get everyone on track if that happened, and I only see my kids once a week for art. I decided to trust him. "J., what do the icons mean to you today?"

J. shared that he had been thinking about the icons for a while. He said that in the hands he saw a Black hand and a White hand and that it reminded him of Dr. Martin Luther King's "I Have A Dream" speech where, in his words, "little Black boys and little Black girls and little White boys and little White girls will work together and get along." J. then said that the brain meant "think about your actions" and the heart meant "no matter how alone or down you feel, you are not alone because God loves you."

I had shivers. The class was silent. I thanked J. for sharing and we got to work painting that day.

I made a point to talk with J. after class to let him know how insightful and brave he was to share. I told him that he showed great leadership qualities, and I saw how he was working to make positive choices in class. "Is it okay if I share what you said with your mom?" I asked him. "Sure, I guess … " he said.

I couldn't wait to send the email to his mom. I shared what J. has said in class and thanked her for all she was doing to support him. This was her reply:

> *"Wow... I'm speechless..... That is great news to me. I am honored to know that he has leadership qualities at a young age. Thank you for sharing this with me. I have forwarded your email to family, friends, and our pastor. Thank you again."*

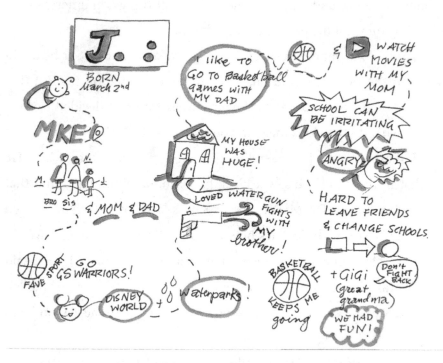

Figure 2. J.'s Sketchnote 1.

J. continued to share what he knew about Black history and I could tell he was interested in it, as well as outraged by what he knew and was learning. I made a point to check in with him and he would often share new information he had watched. I asked him one day if he would mind if we met and talked about his story: where he was born, his best memories, the people in his life, the lessons he learned, anything he wanted to share. I also asked if I could *sketchnote* it, explaining that many times when I sketchnote a conversation with someone, it can be another way of being heard. He was up for it. What he shared is illustrated in Figures 2 and 3.

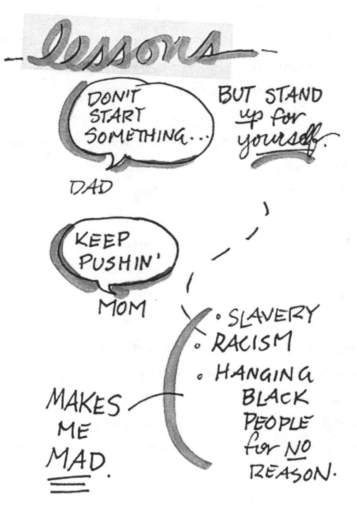

Figure 3. J.'s Sketchnote 2.

J. had again trusted me enough to share how he was feeling. I asked what he thought we could do about the things he listed that make him mad and he shrugged his shoulders. "Do you think you are already doing something pretty powerful and brave by just talking about it with me, a White person?" I asked. "It's a way that I can understand you more and hear about what it's like to be you—to feel your lived experience."

J. was quiet for a bit, and we both sat in the silence before the bell rang.

The following week, J. was restless again when he came into the art room. I had a quote and a picture of Jesse Owens on the board. Once again, J. raised his hand when I asked if anyone knew who the pictured man was. The majority of White students admitted they didn't know anything about Jesse Owens. J. shared that he knew he was a track star at Ohio State University and that he had faced racism from members of the football team because he was Black. When I asked how he knew this, he said, "I watched a movie about it, called *Race*."

I leaned into the conversation and asked the class why they thought they didn't know about Jesse Owens, even though he had broken world records and won four gold medals in the 1936 Olympics. After a few guesses, one student timidly said, "… because of the color of his skin?" We had a conversation about who might be writing the headlines or textbooks that we learn historical facts from and how it is important to ask questions about what voices might not be heard in those texts.

I teach art, so we had to get to making art that day, but I have continued to feel things shift for the better between J. and me. The question I keep in mind with all of my students is not "Are you smart?," but "How are you smart?" J. is smart in confidence, curiosity around Black history, and leadership skills. Some days it feels like two steps forward and one step back for both of us. Even so, I will continue to encourage him to keep learning, questioning, and sharing his lived experience and knowledge like the true positive leader I know he has the potential to become.

SHERRILL KNEZEL is an elementary art educator, graphic recorder, and sketchnoter in Wisconsin who believes that the most important skills her students learn in her classroom are being brave enough to make mistakes and curious enough to see where those mistakes take them. Sherrill has written articles for *EdWeek* on the power of visual note-taking in the classroom as a means to increase personal agency and differentiation. She loves reading, creating daily drawings, being with family, and spending time in, around, or near water.

Social Action Story Activity for "Listening to J."

Sketching Our Strengths

This activity asks you to consider how building a practice of drawing-as-story can help you learn about your strengths individually and in community. For those of us who don't consider ourselves strong artists, drawing like this can be a powerful way to discover our own strengths and ideas as we celebrate those of others.

With a partner, set a timer for three minutes. In that time, diagram or draw out one of the things at which you excel. Reset the timer, again for three minutes, and diagram or draw out one way you think your partner is competent.

Share out and discuss how it felt to name and visualize one of your own areas of intelligence and have someone else name and visualize one part of their experience of your intelligence.

REFLECTIONS ON MARKERS OF JUSTICE AND INJUSTICE

Kevin D. Cordi

There is often social action in standing still, in slowing down. Too often we are quick to take a snapshot of an event, person, or place, but perhaps we need to put down the camera and take in what we see. In this story, Kevin's initial irritation about a no-photos rule at the National Memorial for Peace and Justice turns to gratitude.

There is a popular phrase that says, "a picture is worth a thousand words." However, I questioned if this was accurate after standing in line waiting to enter the recently opened Legacy Museum and, later, the National Memorial for Peace and Justice in Montgomery, Alabama.

Upon entering the Legacy Museum, visitors were told: "no photos allowed." In the expanding line of educators, I heard people grumble about this rule, myself included, and truly did not understand why until I entered these museums.

In this fast-paced 'snap a shot' instant-picture time, we don't slow down. It is a time when we carelessly snap a picture of food or take a selfie, thinking we can capture time in these fast snaps of our phone's camera. A time in which we have hundreds and perhaps thousands of photos stored on disks or computers, which we often forget because of the enormity and the invisibility. It is no exaggeration to say thousands of photos are stored on my phone and my computer—and I rarely look back at them. Taking a picture has become a reflex action.

Because I could not take photos entering the Legacy Museum, I had to slow down and allow my memory to record the experience rather than relying upon the camera's disposable memory.

I took time to see jars with names on them. I took time to wonder about the jar labeled "Otis Price, Perry, FL, August 9, 1938." I saw hundreds of jars next to it with other names, marking the lives that were stolen by the awful practice known as lynching. The collective soil told many stories.

I stopped to read the stark advertisements that provided discounts for buying African American flesh and blood at a slave auction. The advertisement was written as casually as a coupon for a gallon of milk. Human life discounted—a travesty.

I slowed down to see countless images of racial injustice, including personal letters from men who were tortured. I read cries from people searching for family members stolen from them under cover of night. I read the pain in scribbled words in the letters that asked, "Have you seen my brother, he is six-foot-one, they took him." I saw the too-lifelike video image of a woman asking me, "Can you help me find my children?"

There were so many stories there. However, one needed to pause to see and to listen to them, such as the story of Anthony Ray Hinton, who asked, "What would you do if someone took your life away and gave you a death sentence?" It revealed his innocence. He was robbed of a complete life. No one apologized for the theft. I wrote his words down. They were powerful, memorable words. When I continue to teach pre-service educators and teach in schools, I need to share Ray's words. I need to stand still to remember them. I need to let the story stand. A picture on a camera could not do it, because I needed to process them *in the moment* to understand their power.

As I left the Legacy Museum, I saw a parade of framed images of civil rights champions from the past and the present. One was Dolores Huerta. She was a powerful woman advocating for migrant farmers' rights. I taught where Dolores and César Chávez worked, in the fields of the Central Valley in California, and I heard her speak. I remember meeting an elementary school cook after one of my students sang a song about César at our school. She said "I knew this man" to my students, wiping the tears from her eyes, and "can we talk?" Dolores's image brought back this story. As I left, I determined not to leave such strong stories behind. I knew that I would keep the memory of the museum close to me so I could tell the stories.

The stories continued as the group traveled to the National Memorial for Peace and Justice. This place stands as a testament to lives stolen but not forgotten. Each marker told a story. There were too many names on each metal marker. I read that more than 4,000 Black people were lynched between 1877 and 1950.

I stopped at the marker for Ohio, my home state. There were too many names on that marker. I did not want to take a picture, knowing my home state was responsible.

They allowed pictures at the National Memorial for Peace and Justice. I saw people smiling, whole families beside the markers. But their smiles didn't seem right to me. A smile seems to sidestep the tragedy. Although I took many pictures, I brought home even more memories. I was almost the last to leave because the exhibits were so numerous, and the testimonies of people inspired me to learn and tell.

Too often, the inside of classrooms and the detached presentations in textbooks are the pictures of history that we leave students. It is not enough. We need to take our students to the stories. To our classes, we can bring a survivor of a war to speak. We can travel to a local museum and even stand with our students in cemeteries where sacrifices made differences. Remind them to put away their cameras. Instead, teach them to slow down, to take home the memory.

Standing still among those memory markers in Alabama reminded me to make time to remember, to recall, and to educate by telling what I see and why it is there. As an educator, I found out that the saying "a picture is worth a thousand words" is not exactly what was said; instead, this quote is attributed to Frederick R. Barnard, a publisher who said, "One look is worth a thousand words." He attributes it to a Japanese saying. As an educator, I did more than gaze: I searched, stopped, and looked for the stories. Now I feel the words are starting to reveal how I will tell of the experience.

KEVIN CORDI, PH.D. serves as an Assistant Professor at Ohio University Lancaster. For over twenty-five years, he has told stories as a professional storyteller in more than forty states, England, Japan, Singapore, Scotland, and Qatar. He has been, according to the National Storytelling Network, the "first full-time high school storytelling teacher in the country." Kevin is the author of *Playing with Stories: Story Crafting for Writers, Teachers, and Other Imaginative Thinkers* (Parkhurst Brothers, 2014), *Tomorrow's Storytellers Today* (Parkhurst Brothers, 2021) and *You Don't Know Jack: A*

Storyteller Goes to School (University of Mississippi Press, 2019). Everywhere he goes, he now stands still, taking it all in, so he can remember and tell about it.

Social Action Story Activity for
"Reflections on Markers of Justice and Injustice"
Standing Still

We are often in too much of a hurry when we should slow down and be still. There is a rich history of social action work. Many stories wait for us to learn and tell.

Visit a place with social justice history. It can be a museum, a particular place or marker, a space where social justice conversations or events have happened in the past. Be an observer. Take in everything you hear, see, or otherwise experience actively. Take the time to listen to what the walls, signs, people, and simply the place has to tell you. Avoid using your phone or camera.

During or just after your visit, you might handwrite a bulleted list of ideas to build a story or the first draft of a story to help you understand the place or event. Then, talk out or write out the story that you experienced. Write and recall enough to help provide you with a direction for using the story and its teachings in your own life.

Stand still more often. Take time to soak in places that could be story spaces. Instead of rushing, slow down to listen to what the space has to share. Listen to the many voices that speak to story.

COLLABORATION: WORKING IN COMMUNITY FOR CHANGE

SOCIAL ACTION CAN BE LONELY AND DRAINING. Working in community with others provides the support, affirmation, and collective agency often necessary to produce change in our communities and schools. In this section, we learn how educators saw the need for community action against injustice and began that work with their colleagues. We see a *story-care practitioner* leverage the strength of community to provide care to vulnerable in-patients. And we learn how community organizers worked together with low-income workers in rural Minnesota to coordinate transportation services. We also hear a cautionary tale of what happens when educators fail to meet a student's needs while adhering to the structures built to support him.

"WE WANT TO WORK. HELP US GET THERE."

LOREN NIEMI

How do we stand shoulder-to-shoulder with others to work towards our collective freedom? Here, Loren shares a powerful model of how activists can collaborate on advocacy messaging that speaks to the core values of a group and resonates on multiple levels with broader audiences.

THAT PHRASE SEEMS SIMPLE ENOUGH. Easy to remember—and the truth of it is those eight words provided the core message of a rural Minnesota "poor people's" campaign to improve their transportation options.

My partner, James Trice, and I had been hired by the Blandin Foundation to provide civic engagement training with low-wealth individuals in the Grand Rapids, Minnesota area. When we met with them, I noticed that one participant had trouble concentrating, and I asked what was wrong. He needed to go to a dentist for a bad tooth but couldn't. The cost? Yes, but more so that he didn't have a car and needed a ride to the reservation health services.

When we asked if that was an issue for others, it became clear that reliable transportation was an issue for everyone in the room. Cars that broke down, lack of public transit, and inability to afford insurance or tickets issued by the local police all contributed to keeping people from work, health services, kids' school activities, or civic life.

In that moment, this became the focus of our work. What would it take to provide these people with better transportation options? They had ideas ranging from improving the local bus service, extending the school bus service to also taking community members to town, sharing cars (a kind of "proto-Uber" using a phone tree as most of them at that time did not have computers or smartphones), and low-cost or cooperative car repairs.

But before we got to detailing the solutions, we collaborated on an analysis of values and views within their community, using the considerations described in Figure 4.

We began with four boxes, as shown in Figure 1: what we say about ourselves, what others in our community or audience say about themselves, what the others say about us, and finally, what we say about them. The first two boxes are focused on the positives. The second two reflect the prejudices and negatives. It was easy for participants to fill in what others said about them and they about others, but more challenging for them to list what they say about themselves or what are the positives others say about themselves.

As we filled in the positives on both sides, James and I underlined or connected those that reflected the same views or values. Establishing these connections is a crucial step, as messaging ideally should reflect positives on both sides and answer or counter the negatives others say about us. Abbreviating the process, it looks like this: *They say we are lazy* is countered by *we want to work.*

**Message Framing Considerations Used To Develop
"We want to work. Help us get there."**

We want our messages to be:

     1. **Clear** – easy to say and easy to understand

     2. **Concise** – short (can be an 8 second sound bite)

     3. **Compelling** – has a sense of emotional urgency

We'll begin by identifying the positive and negative characteristics of both our own organization/group (framed as 'us' in the chart below) and the perception of those whom we are trying to reach ('them'). Be honest in this step, for it is critical to the message framing process.

Positive things we say about ourselves	Positive things they say about themselves
Prejudiced or negative things we say about them	Prejudiced or negative things they say about us

From the identified positives and negatives, we can choose which statements to focus on to counter negatives or accentuate positives within the message. Looking for the message **invites the audience to respond positively and, ideally, take action—whether** to donate time or money, vote, or pass the message along. To do so, we focus on these elements within the message.

     1. **Connected** – identify/respond to the self-interest of each party

     2. **Contrast** – the positions, reinforce the positives or counter the negatives

     3. **Credible** – it is believable (factually and emotionally)

     4. **Consistent** – even when presented as a variation of a theme

Good messages are memorable in and of themselves, and great messages are metaphoric. They speak to larger images and experiences in the world.

Figure 4. Framing considerations. Adapted from Wellstone Action (2013).

The group had several other mutual affirmations, including *we are church-going people* and *we love our kids*. Still, they agreed that these were secondary statements in relation to the transportation issue. Work was deemed to be the most important statement to make. This became the first part of the message—in effect, the statement of the problem. Now we needed to complete the message by inviting participation in a solution. Once we arrived at *help us get to work*, it seemed obvious.

What is the value of this message if it does not identify a specific answer? This is actually the value because an open-ended message invites participation without limiting it to a single answer. The group could use each idea for any of their possible solutions. We want to work—help us by expanding public transportation services. We want to work—let us ride the school bus to town. We want to work—help us finance a cooperative auto repair service. It offers a straightforward statement of value (we want to work) coupled with an equally simple invitation to resolve an issue.

Once the group had framed this central message, James and I could then walk them through the various civic engagement mechanisms they might participate in: school board, city council, county board, local churches, nonprofits and programs, the state legislature, the federal government, and the various departments and state or federal programs that impacted their lives. Which ones might they approach to develop transportation solutions? Who would speak for them regarding the issues? Which ones would be likely partners? Which ones had the power to act? And in what time frames? What could they do on their own?

Knowing the possibilities, the group began to make plans for what they thought would be the easiest solution to implement—the coop auto repair program—while trying to work with the county, state, and federal programs to expand public transportation options that would serve not only low-wealth individuals and families, but the elderly, those too young to drive, and even tourists.

The crafting of a message seems small, but it is an essential step in making change. It can be a metaphor or a rallying cry. It can provide a "seed" for knowing who we are, what we value, or where we want to go.

Reference
Wellstone Action (2013). Politics the Wellstone way: How to elect progressive candidates and win on issues. United States: University of Minnesota Press.

LOREN NIEMI is a storyteller, advocacy messaging consultant/trainer and author whose work includes *The New Book of Plots* (Parkhurst Brothers, 2012) on narrative forms; *Point of View and the Emotional Arc of Stories*, (Parkhurst Brothers, 2020) co-authored with Nancy Donoval; and *Inviting the Wolf In: Thinking About Difficult Stories*, (August House, 2006) co-authored with Elizabeth Ellis.

Social Action Story Activity for
"We Want to Work. Help Us Get There."
Framing Your Message

Loren's story shows us a simple but powerful method for framing a message for social change. Try it on an issue of importance to you, paying careful attention to the positives you generate.

Remember that it's worth taking the time to listen carefully to the themes and values that participants identify, both for themselves and for the "opposition," to see what resonates below the easy and cliche. The group described in Loren's story spent well over an hour talking through possible messages before settling on the one core value upon which to base their story. Also be aware that the first thing you land on might be a symptom of an even deeper problem. Before treating the symptom by crafting a message and campaigning around it, it's worth asking what underlying problem the group needs to address.

If you do happen to be working individually for this activity, consider finding a thinking partner, even if your core values or issues aren't the same, who can ask questions and provide their perspective.

STOP WAITING

Brittany Brazzel

Some of the most significant movements and changes to education and other socio-political spaces have come from someone saying, "Today, I'll start this!" In this story, Brittany harnesses this attitude to work powerfully in the community, in particular making visible the voices of students in her school who have been the victims of racist comments from teachers and other students.

My first in-service day as a brand-new teacher was a whirlwind. Upon arriving at the high school, I met my assigned coach, and we went right into the thick of introductions.

"Finally, some diversity," a colleague from another school said while taking my hand for a shake. "It's about time!"

In hindsight, I should have taken this comment and the many I received after as something more, but I brushed it off as excitement. The district was hiring more people of color; nothing wrong with that. As the morning continued and more people interacted with me, the reality of my situation began to sink in. I stuck out like a sore thumb. By the end of the day, I felt like a commodity.

After arriving home for the night, I immediately went online and began searching for my district's staff demographics. The anxiety of not having this register with me all summer started to wash over me with each link I clicked. I grew up in a neighboring town and knew the district was small, rural, and very white, but could I really be the only Black teacher? When I finally found the stats, my fear was confirmed. Under full-time employee—teacher, the result was one: me.

I went upstairs to be alone and process. I journaled these thoughts: *"I have this feeling I've become the poster child for diversity in a school that's greatly lacking."* A month later: *"I don't feel at home when I'm working. I feel myself shutting down and closing off. Regret."* My K-12 experiences had followed me into adulthood, and I was feeling isolated and alone. What had I gotten myself into?

I spent most of the first semester talking myself off the ledge. Thank goodness for the students! They truly are a life source, and they helped keep my mindset in check. After all, I'm used to being one of the only, if not the only, person of color in spaces. Why would this be different?

So I started to monitor the microaggressions hurled my way, day to day. I honestly thought I could help or change them. I had not yet learned this was not my responsibility or burden to bear.

Keeping up with the day-to-day rigor of my first year had me at new levels of exhaustion. Yet teaching also brought a new sense of joy. For the first time professionally, I was doing exactly what I was meant to be doing. However, the reality of how much time is needed to make meaningful change within the system overtook me; I needed to step back and refocus.

I decided to use the rest of the year to 'learn' my co-workers and create deeper connections. Problems arose almost immediately. The more comfortable people started to feel around me, the more intense the microaggressions. I did not yet have a toolbox of strategies, language, or the resilience to consistently disrupt and educate repeat offenders. Worse yet, instead of working to build those strong relationships, I began to pull away. Shouldn't they know better?

By the fourth quarter, I had found a small squad. I used their support for my I-can't-wait-to-quit-and-leave-the-profession days and discussed philosophical ideas and the potential impediments to bringing them to fruition. Through these connections, I started to understand the cultural heart of my school and district. I learned that the average years of service is at fifteen, and a large chunk of our staff once walked the very halls they now teach in. "Old school" perfectly summarizes the vibe. A sense of pride and the determination to keep things the same thrived. This became, and still is, my unstoppable barrier. It is almost impossible to invoke change when you can't be taken seriously because you're a freshman teacher or because your eagerness to produce radical change incites fear.

I spent the first few weeks of summer break decompressing, doing everything to forget my profession. My escape is through books; the last title I grabbed from the library before leaving for the year was a copy of *Just Mercy* by Bryan Stevenson. *Just Mercy* was not the first, second, or third book I read that summer, but when I finally read it, my world was rocked. Why didn't I know about this level of injustice, this level of oppression? I felt pitted, empty, and angry—what else didn't I know? I had obtained a history degree having only learned a tiny percentage of actual history. With a new curiosity sparked, I spent the next summer month dedicated to relearning stolen and lost knowledge; my journey to awareness had begun.

When August hit, I felt like a new me. I was stronger in my conviction to change the education system and dedicated to implementing action with a social justice lens. I refused to work at a school that whitewashed history, suppressed oppressed perspectives, and denied truth and reality from its students. The urge to awaken my colleagues and break the mold of normalcy by kick-starting their journeys to awareness fueled me.

Along with one White colleague, I introduced a new committee to staff during our first meeting. We called it the Cultural Diversity Committee (CDC) and set a goal to create a dedicated group of staff that worked to "respect and embrace diversity through the common goals of developing, educating, and increasing cultural awareness and responsiveness within the walls of our school." My personal goal for the year was to create moments or opportunities which could open the eyes of staff to the daily realities of our students, especially our marginalized students.

Our first actionable moment fell into our laps after students from a neighboring university had begun to unpack the volume of microaggressions students were experiencing on campus. Their visual campaign sparked conversation and controversy, so we took their campaign framework and made it our own. We began by asking students of color to use a small whiteboard to write down examples of microaggression directed at them, making sure the comments or actions had happened during school hours. We then wanted to take a picture of each student holding their board to create a visual slideshow to share with the staff.

Initially, the students wanted no part. Fear and angst spilled from each student we asked:

"Will other students see this?"

"What if the staff gets upset?"

"What if staff comes for us?"

They were scared, and rightly so. The gravity of what we were asking them to do had sunk in. In order to protect them, we ensured their anonymity and only took pictures of their hands holding the whiteboard.

Can't you find me weed? You're Black!

But you look White, not Asian.

You speak Spanish?! But you're so white.

Why don't you have a normal name?

You sound like a girl. Fag.

You don't act like Black people usually do.

When we presented the slides to staff during a mandatory meeting, you could have heard a pin drop. There was zero preparation and no warning before slowly and silently scrolling through thirty slides, each displaying a single example of hate. At the subsequent CDC meeting, attendance was up, eyes were opened, and the want to change was present.

With interest in our committee growing, our next step was to start facilitating and encouraging difficult conversations. To accomplish this safely and organically, we decided to start and run a staff book club. We selected *Why Are All The Black Kids Sitting Together in the Cafeteria?* by Beverly Daniel Tatum; it was education-focused (for our data people) and contained several open-ended questions that could ignite conversations many weren't accustomed to or were afraid of having.

Twenty staff members met once a month and had tough conversations, shared their re-learning, and began to plan for action and accountability. As the year went on and as more staff began to explore and converse, you could feel the culture shift within our building. Over the next three years, staff involvement increased, causing us to add *White Like Me* by Tim Wise and *Blindspot: Hidden Biases of Good People* by Anthony Greenwald and Mahzarin Banaji to our book list for professional development.

As the original book club was wrapping up with the end of the year, I had one more awareness element I wanted staff to experience before summer: a student panel consisting of only students of color. I needed our staff to hear their voices, see the pain, and begin to understand how difficult it can be to walk into the building each day. This would not be a Q&A. I directed staff to just listen, telling them we would debrief at a later time. The students had the following four questions ahead of time:

1. Based on your experiences so far, what can you say about cultural diversity within our school?

2. Explain what it means to be a student of color in class.

3. Culturally/racially, what have your challenges been while at school?

4. What can staff do to help make your experiences better or more engaging? How can we help overcome your challenges?

Goodness, I was proud. The students displayed their bravery and confidence with grace as they brought up each example of racism, discrimination, and prejudice. They shared their trauma using painful memories and stories. When tears fell from their eyes, peers stepped up to offer supportive encouragement and side hugs. They held nothing back and gave everything. As a building, this was our pinnacle moment, and you could feel it in the room. We were ready to act.

BRITTANY BRAZZEL is a fierce and enthusiastic addition to education and currently works as a high school history educator. Brittany is determined to create and maintain inclusive educational equity through leadership, student voice, and curriculum. She has presented her ideas and progress at conferences throughout Wisconsin and digitally connects with educators across the United States for expanded learning. Brittany holds a B.A. in history and an M.Ed. from Edgewood College.

Social Action Story Activity for "Stop Waiting"
Visual Communication of Community Experiences

In Brittany's story, students recounting discriminatory language in their own handwriting provides the first actionable moment for a school's growing racial justice movement. The power comes not just from the words themselves but also from the visual nature of the project.

In this activity, you'll brainstorm how you might find avenues for communicating the experiences of communities of people who are affected by an issue of concern to you. Some inspiration:

- Have community members create artwork about the issue, perhaps accompanied by short artist's statements.

- Collect quotes or poems by community members about the issue, then have them printed on large paper for effective display.

- Create a video or photo series of interviews about an issue.

You'll also need a plan for displaying the work and stories of community members. Public libraries often have a gallery wall, as do coffee shops and government buildings. You might also find a news outlet, a popular blog, or a podcast interesting in amplifying the voices of community members.

Your team might also consider the activity **"Framing Your Message"** following **"We Want to Work. Help Us Get There."** Done in tandem, these two exercises can build strong momentum in your community and help collaborators deliberately focus on specific messages if appropriate.

Other tips for organizing visual communications of community experiences:

- If you are editorializing in any way (for example, by editing others' writing or storytelling), make sure to do so with the writers/speakers/artists directly. We must provide each other the dignity to have agency over the presentation of our own stories or experiences. This is especially critical when those stories may make us vulnerable.

Consider opportunities for anonymity, as Brittany does for her students in the handwriting project.

DIFFICULT CONVERSATIONS

Beverly Stuckwisch

Sometimes, working in community requires us to work on ourselves first. Here, Bev shows us the power of building our own capacity to engage in what we perceive to be difficult conversations through reflection with a trusted community—and how cycles of communication in community can slowly increase understanding when groups are being marginalized or placed at risk.

I STILL FEEL LIKE A NOVICE TEACHER IN MANY WAYS, but I have always felt strongly about my ability to advocate for students. In fact, student advocacy was promoted highly in my teacher preparation program and is an expectation for teacher evaluation in Ohio, where I live and teach. To build up that advocacy, a colleague and I helped students start the first gender and sexuality alliance (GSA) at our small, rural high school located in a politically conservative community. We had excellent support from our principal. In fact, his daughter was the original president of the group.

At first, the GSA was primarily a social group—a place where LGBTQ+ students and allies could come once a week to be themselves without fear of judgment. The group's existence spread by word of mouth and by public address announcements, even though many of the students had no idea what the GSA initials represented. As that safe space began to develop and students were able to identify allies within the school, participants also began to develop a desire for more visibility and activism.

Two years into its existence, the GSA organized a recognition of the Day of Silence, "a student-led national event where folks take a vow of silence to highlight the silencing and erasure of LGBTQ+ people at school" (GLSEN, 2018) in April. Participation was voluntary, and the GSA set up a table in the cafeteria for students to sign up. Over 70 students participated in that initial year.

While the students, my colleague, and I anticipated negative comments and pushback from some community members, other issues arose that we did not predict. For example, a parent called the principal and complained that some GSA students had been going up to lunch tables informing people of the event, thus forcing the topic of homosexuality on her child. Another parent was concerned that her child would be "forced to be silent for gay rights," which was neither true nor an accurate depiction of the event's purpose.

Because of incidents like these, we recognized a need to be more transparent in our advertising of the event, perhaps appealing to individuals' empathy by highlighting the disproportionate bullying, suicide, and murder rates for LGBTQ+ students. However, because of the parent concerns, the principal asked that students tone down the advertisement altogether—specifically by not going from table to table in the lunchroom and instead allowing interested students to come to them. The day of the event came and went without too many issues. Students mentioned hearing some homophobic and transphobic slurs in the hallways, but in general, felt the event was a success.

Feeling more empowered by the fall of the next school year, the GSA students set their focus on making themselves more visible in the community. They knew some students either didn't know about the group, weren't allowed to attend, or weren't ready to come out. They wanted to let those students know they weren't alone. As a result, their next project was to create a compilation of the pride flags they felt represented their identities, drawn and colored by hand. Each flag would represent a student in the GSA, so the sheer number of flags would send the message they intended.

Because of the issues the previous year, I took a photo of the finished flag (Figure 5) and sent it to the principal for approval prior to hanging. Once we had that approval, it went up in a large blank space of the math hallway (somewhere we knew all students would pass at some point in their day). Two days later, my colleague and I were asked to meet with the principal during our lunch period. I felt sick to my stomach because I knew what the outcome of that meeting would be—the flag was coming down.

Figure 5. Compilation pride flag colored by GSA students.
Photo credit: Beverly Stuckwisch

The principal had been contacted by some parents, students, and at least one staff member who expressed issues with the flag. While he responded with defense to remarks that were flat-out discriminatory, he found himself stuck on some other issues raised. For example, the third flag from the right on the bottom row included the word "pansexual." Some parents expressed they did not want the school to be educating their children on sexuality in any form and that the word itself hanging on the wall was in fact attempting to educate students on multiple sexualities. It was also brought to light that the school policies currently in place did not allow "non-curriculum groups" to hang flyers and posters inside the school. Although that hadn't been enforced in the recent past, it would have to be enforced now, starting with taking the flag down.

My response was angry tears. I knew how much it meant to the GSA students and what taking it down would represent to them and those who've oppressed them. At the time, I was so emotional that I was unable to process my principal's response or address it with him in an effective way. Instead, I let my feelings stew and blamed him harshly for not being able to see the future and predict what would happen when the flag went up. As someone who historically avoided conflict, it took nearly six months for me to feel like I could have an honest conversation with him again.

The 2016 presidential election followed closely behind the flag incident. Students expressed concern and fear in GSA meetings. There was a rising tension in the air as transgender restroom rights were questioned throughout the nation. In April 2017, the GSA sponsored the Day of Silence again. Because of their inability to advertise in ways the students felt were effective, they had about half the number of participants as the previous year. The students, my colleague, and I felt stifled in how we could support activist work in the community, while at the same time feeling it was more important than ever. I found myself making blanket assumptions about colleagues and community members that I knew to be politically conservative.

At a Knowles Teacher Initiative meeting, I expressed all of these feelings to a small group of other Knowles Fellows. It was in this setting that I was challenged to reconsider my assumptions. We identified a common thread of not knowing how to address difficult conversations in each of our settings. As a result, we decided to read *Difficult Conversations* (Stone et al., 2010) and make it a goal to face those issues head-on.

In the final week of the 2016–2017 school year, I worked with my principal to host an open conversation about the GSA. The principal, superintendent, guidance counselors, about ten staff members, five students from the GSA, and one parent attended. Prior to the conversation, I emailed a document to staff and GSA students outlining the purpose of the conversation, as well as some conversation starters. The purpose was to:

- ensure that students and staff were on the same page about the purpose of the GSA,

- help make the conversation about the GSA more positive in the community, and

- give a voice to anyone who had concerns or comments about the purpose of the GSA.

Initiating this conversation felt risky to me. I worried that either no one would attend or that someone would derail the conversation. I think that was the biggest reason why I waited until the end of the year. If it went well, we would be starting the new year with some footing. If it didn't go well, we'd have the summer to recover and work on next steps. Figure 6 shows a visual representation of how the conversation went.

After the meeting, I felt like our conversation accomplished exactly what we hoped it would. Once everything was out in the open, it was clear that the more vocal staff members who were in opposition to some of the GSA's activities did not understand the students' situations or motives. At the beginning of the meeting, one staff member stated that if LGBTQ+ students in our school were being bullied, then it was their responsibility to stand up for themselves and to report it. More than one person reached out to me after the meeting, referring to his comments as *victim-blaming*.

However, one thing that was clear in the conversation was that this staff member had never considered how difficult it would be for a student to advocate for themselves when no one else was advocating for them. More than one staff member was shocked to learn that some of those students had limited support at home and that a few had even been kicked out of their homes. Most importantly, some good ideas came up for moving forward and creating a more inclusive learning environment for the next year, as shown in Figure 6.

Another, more personal, result of this conversation was that I was finally able to start to see some different perspectives. Planning events solely focused on the GSA and on LGBTQ+ topics was further isolating those students in the eyes of some community members. Such isolation was something neither the students in the GSA nor I had considered. Even if we disagreed with how some people responded, we couldn't make progress until we at least recognized their feelings and concerns.

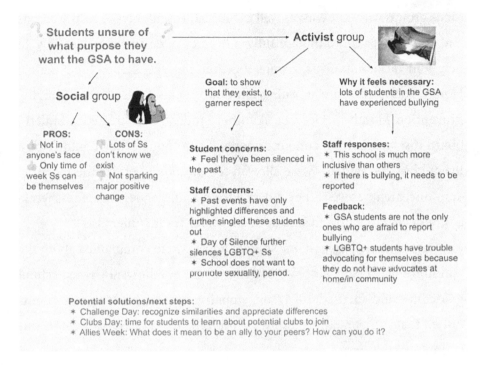

Figure 6. Takeaways from the open conversation about the GSA.
Image credit: Beverly Stuckwisch

Moving forward, we wanted to focus more on partnering with other groups to help create a more inclusive community for all students. I hoped that through these projects, more students who needed the GSA would find it, and other students would discover ways to stand up for their peers as allies. If one of the major goals of the GSA was to help students feel less alone and isolated in our school, then perhaps partnering with other groups to work on bigger projects and goals would accomplish just that.

At the beginning of the 2017–2018 school year, I reached out to all staff to create a professional learning community (PLC) to examine the culture of our school and our students' experiences of harassment and bullying. Fourteen staff members joined the group, as well as four students. We met throughout the year, analyzing data from surveys, interviews, and focus groups with students, as well as brainstorming ways to help students and staff engage more thoughtfully on topics of empathy and equity. To help join various students' groups together, the PLC helped the National Honor Society prepare morning announcements for National Bullying Prevention Month in October. Another student club created a bulletin board displaying those announcements. Even though they couldn't post flyers, the GSA students were allowed to continue to utilize the morning announcements as well. They did so during Transgender Awareness week, announcing bullying and suicide statistics for trans students.

As predicted, at least one student and a parent complained about the announcements. Still, since we had made sure to follow all written school guidelines and focused solely on empathy-building for trans students rather than on something more politicized, it was easy to defend our actions.

My colleague and I now work at other schools for reasons unrelated to the challenges we faced advising the GSA. Prior to opening up the conversations I had previously been avoiding, I would have wrongly assumed that there were very few support systems for the GSA students other than my colleague and me. Instead, when we announced that we were leaving, two other teachers volunteered to be the advisors moving forward. Several others voiced support as well. Additionally, the city the school serves hosted its first pride event in the summer of 2018. One of the GSA students even attended a planning meeting for the event, which led to a table display representing our school.

Looking back, I genuinely feel that my fear and unwillingness to have uncomfortable and emotionally charged discussions was one of the biggest things preventing the positive change I desired. Using difficult conversations to unpack my assumptions about people I perceived to have different values than mine was the first step to real change.

References

GLSEN, Inc. (2018). GLSEN's day of silence. Retrieved from https://www.glsen.org/day-silence

Stone, D., Patton, B., & Heen, S. (2010). *Difficult conversations: How to discuss what matters most.* New York, N.Y: Penguin Books.

BEVERLY STUCKWISCH graduated from Michigan State University with a B.S. in chemistry and a Master's in education. She currently teaches math at Dublin Coffman High School, where she has also co-supervised Spectrum, the school's gender and sexuality alliance. Beverly also works as an Associate Editor for *Kaleidoscope: Educator Voices and Perspectives.*

Social Action Story Activity for "Having Difficult Conversations"
Building your capacity for risk

So often, we shy away from difficult conversations. For each of us, there may be many reasons why we choose to avoid tense and uncomfortable situations with others. But as we see in Bev's story, difficult conversations are just one of the necessary steps to working toward inclusive and equitable communities. So what is it that makes such discussions difficult for you?

First, reflect on a recent experience where you avoided conflict or a difficult conversation. Why did you avoid it? What did you sense was risky about the conversation? What were you worried might happen?

Now, think about having that difficult conversation. What is important to the person or persons with whom you would like to talk? What common goals or ideals do you have that you might build on?

Time to get ready! Find a trusted colleague or friend and ask them to partner with you to role-play this conversation. If they're unfamiliar with the problem and people at hand, give your partner enough information to play the other person's role.

It's essential for your partner to work to play this role with respect for the real person they are representing, without stereotyping or portraying this person as an enemy.

Try out a worst-case scenario and a best-case scenario. The more genuine and realistic the role-play, the better!

Reflect on this experience. What did you learn about yourself? What new insights do you have about this situation that will help you have this difficult conversation?

STORM-STAYED: STORYTELLING IN A GERIATRIC PSYCHIATRY WARD

Dan Yashinsky

For geriatric psychiatry patients, using stories and storytelling to address the feeling of being "storm-stayed"—held in place by conditions outside your control—can be a powerful treatment. Dan shares how "story-care" helps these patients "reclaim their sense of wonder and suspense— and, surprisingly, laughter—even in the midst of their suffering."

IN CAPE BRETON, NOVA SCOTIA, if a blizzard keeps you in your neighbor's house, they say you've been "storm-stayed." Since I first learned this term from a storyteller in the Maritimes, it has come to hold special meaning for my work team and me.

I am a storyteller-in-residence at Baycrest Health Sciences, a research and teaching hospital for the elderly in Toronto. My work here, known as "storycare," reflects Baycrest's philosophy that literature and storytelling are essential to healthcare.

Every week, I work with clinicians and therapists to bring storycare to patients in the palliative care, rehab, and long-term-care units. Twice weekly, I head to the fourth floor to co-lead storytelling circles for geri-atric psychiatry patients.

The men and women on the fourth floor suffer from severe depres-sion. They are indeed storm-stayed, and the psychiatry ward is their temporary haven. Many stay on the unit for weeks or months at a time.

Storycare, in this context, means creating a time and space where stories can be told, heard, imagined, and remembered. The patients often tell me that they've lost the threads of their own life stories: They can barely remember their pre-hospital lives and find it hard to imagine what could happen next. On a good day, storycare helps them reclaim their sense of wonder and suspense—and, surprisingly, laughter—even amid their suffering.

Sometimes I bring props to spark new stories. A Russian nesting doll launches stories about our hidden and invisible selves. A small wooden spoon stirs up memories of kitchens and beloved grandmothers.

Once, after telling *Stone Soup*—the traditional folktale about a soup that starts with a stone and ends up nourishing the whole community—we created an imaginary "soup" from ingredients the patients suggested: hope, improved memory, peace, kindness, happiness, energy, deep and restorative sleep.

Another time, I passed around a silk butterfly and asked them to imagine what a caterpillar might say to the butterfly.

"I wish I could fly like you," came one response.

"Be patient," someone replied. "You will, one day. You will become me. You will fly."

Sometimes I tell fairy tales full of adventure, quests, dangers, and transformations. Then, like Scheherazade, I'll stop at the most exciting part and, despite their good-natured protests, leave the next chapter for the following week.

The patients tell me that our storytelling group is a welcome break amid the clinical routine.

"This is a hard place to show strong feelings," someone commented one day. The others concurred. Their illness, and the potent medications they take, can muffle their emotions and silence their words.

As they spoke, I was struck by the sheer—sometimes desperate—bravery it must take to step away from your everyday life and come in for treatment.

"You're far braver than any of the characters in the stories I've been telling you," I said. "I would like to honor you for your courage in being here."

As it happened, one of the patients was an acclaimed writer and educator. Dr. O. had done social justice work around the world.

At the end of our storytelling circle, I asked him if he'd work with me to create an honoring ceremony for the fourth-floor patients. Fragile and ill as he was, he agreed.

At the outset, he and I decided to avoid the terminology of illness and treatment. Instead, we referred to the patients as travelers and to depression as the terrifying, all-consuming storm that had forced them to seek sanctuary.

We often discussed what it meant to be "storm-stayed" in a psychiatric unit. Dr. O. described in heartbreaking detail how his illness had derailed his sense of purpose and belief in himself. Because the fourth-floor unit fosters a strong sense of community, we crafted moments in the ceremony that recognized the ways in which its members support each other.

Dr. O. and I met weekly until we had a draft that we liked, then test-drove it with the group. Afterward, people spoke about how they appreciated being recognized and honored as travelers rather than as patients.

"Travelers have the ability to move on," one said. "They have the hope of new adventures."

The ceremony evolved based on the patients' responses. When it was finished, I began to use the ceremony regularly to open the story-telling circle. Participants often report that the ceremony has given them a new way of understanding both their illness and their journey towards healing.

For Dr. O., writing it became part of his gradual creative reawakening. He has since gone home, but the ceremony is his legacy, a lasting gift for anyone suffering from depression. In his memorable phrase, it affirms that we can "go forth even in darkness" to seek our lost or hidden stories.

In the hope of helping storm-stayed travelers wherever they may be, here is the ceremony:

(Ring a bell to begin)

Invocation

The ceremony we are about to do is an honoring of your life–
of who you are,
who you were,
and who you will become.
We gather to honor your courage in being here,
and to remind ourselves that we are not alone on this journey–
Welcome, Travelers, and thank you for joining this circle

The Storm That Brought You Here

We know the storm that brought you here,

The storm of depression

That takes away your sense of purpose,

Your pleasure in life,

Your ability to move forward.

You are storm-stayed now,

And this can be your sanctuary until you're ready to travel again.

Four Blessings

Here are four blessings for you–

We invite you to respond after each blessing with these words of affirmation: *Let it be so.*

May you find your path of healing through this darkness.

Let it be so.

May you move your life on to new and fulfilling challenges.

Let it be so.

May you gain wisdom from your season with depression.

Let it be so.

May you share your wisdom with others who need it.

Let it be so.

You Are Not Alone

Now that you have found a haven,

You will have an opportunity

To recover what you have lost in the storm

And to one day travel

To new destinations.

You are not alone;

Many have been lost in this storm,

Many have sought shelter here,

Many have traveled again when they were ready.

End of Ceremony

(Ring bell)

With the sound of this bell,

We remember that, though we feel broken,

We will keep trying to mend.

(Ring bell)

With the sound of this bell,

We remember that we may go forth even in darkness.

(Ring bell)

With the sound of this bell,

We thank you for gathering and dream together of the possible wonder of new beginnings.

(Ring bell)

DAN YASHINSKY worked as the storyteller-in-residence at Baycrest Health Sciences, in Toronto, from 2014-2019. He is the author of *Swimming with Chaucer: A Storyteller's Logbook* (Litdistco, 2013) and *Suddenly They Heard Footsteps: Storytelling for the Twenty-First Century* (Knopf, 2010). He also edited the *Baycrest Wisdom Book*, a collection of stories by the center's patients and staff. The Baycrest ceremony has been shared at a Storytelling in Health conference in Swansea, Wales, and with members of the Healing Story Alliance.

Social Action Activity for "Storm-stayed: Storytelling in a Geriatric Psychiatry Ward"

Too often, we wish we had captured the stories of someone before that person left the world. This action celebrates the stories of elders.

For this action, you might take the time to capture a story. Interview an elder and, if possible, talk with people influenced by that person's story. Work together to share the story, either in public (with your interviewee's permission and collaboration) or simply with the person who told it to you. What did you discover? How can your revelations be applied to the social action work you are planning or carrying out?

Alternatively, you might instead take time to learn more deeply about the life and actions of an activist you admire. Consider asking a local librarian for help making sure you're using sources that accurately tell that person's story. For example, the stories we find about Rosa Parks in books and memorials often undercut her preparation and life of social action in favor of a different narrative. Work to seek a more accurate story.

ONE OF THE BEST SCHOOLS IN THE STATE

Ursula Wolfe-Rocca

Social action is not about trying to change something you don't understand. But sometimes, we act as 'wanna-be heroes' and try to change it anyway. Our conviction that we are helping masks the underlying problems of inequality, transforming our good intentions into destructive action while leaving us feeling like we've done all we could. Ursula reminds us that acting for what we perceive as the common good is not always the best choice. (Nathan's name is a pseudonym.)

There are nine overstuffed swivel chairs, chairs that swallow up all sitters, especially the young. Usually, only four or five of the seats around the long, shiny, rectangular table are needed: one for the student, one for a parent, one for the learning specialist, one for a teacher, and one for the odd counselor, administrator, or speech pathologist who may have some relevant input. But today, all the spaces are filled. Today we have bigwig functionaries: the district director of special education, the district school psychologist, the vice-principal. My title is the *cooperating* teacher.

We are here to talk about Nathan, a junior. Nathan isn't in the room yet; soon, he'll be beckoned out of class, sling his backpack over both shoulders, adjust his drawers to just below the lower curve of his rear, shift his cap to sit atop his skull and at an angle, and begin a slow, prideful saunter down to the Alumni Conference Room. The conference room is decorated with framed, circa-1955 photographs of White athletes from this school's illustrious past. Before he arrives, the seven White Professional Educators grouped around the table are discussing Important Matters, like *What Is Really In Nathan's Best Interest* and *Why Does Nathan Squander All This Good Will* and *Is Nathan Smoking Marijuana* and *Is It Time For Alternative Placement.*

Nathan opens the door, and the White Professional Educators greet him, too eagerly for the occasion or the hour. This is the kind of greeting that says, "We very much hope you believe that we are in no way aware or conscious of the fact that you are a Black teenager and we are White Professional Educators. We feel *so* comfortable and at ease!"

Nathan pauses at the head of the table, tightens the cords on his backpack ever so slightly and half-laughs, "Whoa, I don't need all this; I don't want all this. This is scary, yo."

Nervous laughter from the group. The Learning Specialist of Progressive Politics ignores the comment and gets down to The Important Reasons We Are Here.

"Well, Nathan, as you and I have talked about, and as I think everyone here is aware, we are here to talk about your placement in Special Education…."

Nathan has seated himself in the only available chair, next to his diminutive White grandmother with whom he lives. She will be a crucial player in this Important Meeting. Backpack still secured to both shoulders.

Nathan's body, as always, is full of frenetic energy. In class, he has the I-am-being-swarmed-by-mosquitoes twitchiness counterbalanced by the psychic focus of a mathematician at the whiteboard. But here he is more swarmed-by-mosquitoes than mathematician. He says, "Nah, I don't want that. I don't need that."

Meaningful glances pass between the Seven White Professional Educators, glances that say, "We saw *this* coming" and "Heeeeeere we go." Deep breath, through the nostrils, out the nostrils, and the Young Male Vice-Principal Who Listens to Hip Hop leans forward with an authority that conveys to his co-conspirators, "I got this." He speaks slowly, faux-compassionately, oozing *We Only Want What's Best For You.*

"Nathan, we understand that you don't want to be in Special Education, but if you are not Special Ed, you cannot be enrolled in Learning Center, and right now, from what I understand, that is the only place you are getting any work done."

"Nah, nah, nah." Twitch, shift, bob, swivel. "That's not true. I'm getting work done."

With a *You Can't Deny It* matter-of-fact-ness, Another White Professional Educator, this time the School Psychologist Who Lives in North Portland and Is Dating a Black Man, chimes in: "Nathan, I have your current grades right here. You have a 43% in history, a 54% in English, and a 55% in Algebra. The only class you are passing is Learning Center and now you're saying you don't need it."

"I *don't* need it," Nathan mutters, shaking his head.

Now the Director of Special Education is taking a turn. His slow, melodic tone suggests Nathan is a very young child who needs things S-P-E-L-L-E-D out: "Nathan, I want you to hear me, champ. Really listen now, okay? Being in Special Ed does *not* mean you are not intelligent...."

Before he can list all the ways in which *This Will Help You, Nathan*, Nathan interrupts. "I am NOT dumb, man. I am smart! Ask Ms. Wolfe. She knows. I *love* history."

All eyes swing to me. Okay, I am up to bat.

Nathan, you are smart, but this overwhelmingly White establishment is suffocating you. You need to get out. GET OUT. You need to go to a school where you are not a token, a mascot, or the cultural capital of White kids' hip-hop dreams. Right now, there is not a single Black adult in this building. That is not an accident. You are never going to make it here. Get out, Nathan. Get out while there is time to salvage your education, your spirit, your energy, while you still remember how to be the best version of yourself.

But that is not what I say. After all, I am a White Professional Educator.

I say, "Nathan, you are smart, but you're not doing your work, and we'd like you to get some credit for these classes. Being smart is only half the equation." Or maybe I don't say that. Maybe I lean forward in my chair, make eye contact with this child, who has just begged me for some love, and crush him with some equally miss-the-fucking-point-completely statement.

Having rejected the overture of this lonely and outnumbered boy, this sweet, smart, fiery, sensitive, complex boy, I now get lots of appreciative nods from my fellow White Professional Educators and especially from White Grandma who gives me an aggressive "Amen, sister!" look and piles on: "Nathan, that is what I have been telling you. If you don't do the work, your intelligence means jack squat."

The Young Vice Principal Who Speaks With Authority and Listens to Hip Hop speaks again. This time, he's directing his questions to Grandma: "What do you see Nathan doing at home? Is he doing homework? Playing video games? Watching TV?" These are unfair questions since I am pretty sure he already knows the answer. It's a softball to Grandma, so she can hit it out of the park.

"Ha! I wish! He's never *at* home. All he does is take the bus to North Portland and smoke pot with his so-called friends! He'll deny it, but I know that's what he's doing. I *know* it!"

Nathan sucks his teeth, vigorously shaking his head: "Nah, nah, nah. I *don't* deny it. You just don't understand. Those are my friends, my *friends*. How am I supposed to see them if I stay at home all night doing homework?"

Grandmother: "Well, I have told you—those kids are not welcome in my house. And you won't be welcome either if you keep doing drugs."

"I don't care." Nathan desperately repeats this refrain. "I don't care. I don't care. I don't care."

The Seven White Professional Educators sense the *Meeting Regarding Nathan's Future* is careening off-track. Someone attempts to refocus on the *Reason We Are All Here*.

"Well, our purpose today is to make a decision regarding Nathan's eligibility for Special Education..."

Nathan again: "I don't want it. I don't need it. I am not dumb."

Another round of *Why Won't You Listen to Reason* from the Seven White Professional Educators. Another round of *You Just Don't Understand* from Nathan. We have reached a stalemate, an impasse. Neither side can move.

Nathan drops out of school less than six weeks later.

The Seven White Professional Educators continue to work at one of the best schools in the state.

URSULA WOLFE-ROCCA has taught high school social studies since 2000 in a suburb of Portland, Oregon. She writes regularly for *Rethinking Schools* magazine (and sits on its editorial board) and is a teacher organizer/curriculum writer for the Zinn Education Project. Her articles include "My So-Called Public School," "Standing with Standing Rock," and "COINTELPRO: Teaching the FBI's War on the Black Freedom Movement." Ursula teaches, parents, learns, loves, rages, grieves, and dreams toward a different world, imperfectly, but always.

Social Action Activity for "One of the Best Schools in the State"
Reframing to center harm

Ursula's powerful telling story grapples with how White people use the harm they have inflicted upon people of color for their own growth and identity development. Instead of centering the White teachers' redemption, however, Ursula's telling centers the harm inflicted and directly confronts her part in it.

For this action, write or privately record yourself speaking about a time you were complicit in harming someone. Rather than quickly shifting to what you learned or how you grew—both of which are often how such stories are framed in some social justice spaces, particularly by White teachers and activists learning about race and racism—sit with the harm. Acknowledge intense feelings or thoughts that come up and record them.

By developing our abilities to acknowledge and describe the harm we do to others, we are better able to acknowledge and describe when we notice harm done in our social action work, better able to apologize when appropriate, and better able to build a plan for changing our actions. By articulating our way through moments when we have inflicted harm, we also often learn more about our place in the story.

VOICE: SPEAKING "TRUTH" FOR OURSELVES AND OTHERS

THE COURAGE TO SPEAK UP AGAINST INJUSTICE looks different to different people. In this section, we see stories of people speaking up against ignorance and injustice in various spaces and diverse ways. For allies and co-conspirators, surrendering some of our privileges so that others may have the opportunities they are currently denied is part of what it means to speak for change.

RED HATS IN THE BLACK MUSEUM

Sabrina Joy Stevens

When a Black visitor to the Smithsonian National Museum of African American History & Culture views groups of students wearing symbols associated with racist social movements, she finds she has to seek out their adult chaperones and raise the question of whether an adult has spoken to the students about the meaning of the symbols in this space. In this story, Sabrina models what it looks like to speak up against spreading hate while sharing her inner dialogue on the difficulty of doing so and seeking necessary support.

I AM ON A GROUP TRIP TO THE MUSEUM. The Black one. The long-time-coming Black Smithsonian that I, for many frustrating reasons, have not gotten to tour until today. It was a rough morning, but I made it in and am looking forward to a memorable experience. I find a sunny spot to meditate quickly and shift gears, then grab my journal and some pens before catching up with my group for a photo.

As we head down to the bottom floor of the museum, contemplating the horrors of enslavement, I spot a group of police officers a bit ahead of us. I start to say to myself, "Well, at least they're . . ." when I see a fair-skinned officer with a "Blue Lives Matter" flag and a Gadsden flag patch on his backpack. He, a current participant in our country's system of mass incarceration, spawned from this very history of enslavement, is blithely walking into *this* museum wearing a symbol of resistance to the very idea that police should be held accountable for abusing and murdering Black people in cold blood.

I take a deep breath and walk over. "Hey. So you're here, as a police officer, wearing a Blue Lives Matter patch in *this* space. I just wanted to say that I hope you learn something today." He responds with a simultaneously surprised and genial "Thank you!" I smile tightly and walk away.

I float in and back out of our group and continue taking in the museum on my own. It starts to get more crowded, including lots of school tour groups. For a museum on a weekday, the crowds seemed appropriate until I started seeing groups of mostly White middle school students (you guessed it! Including some in MAGA hat !) bouncing and giggling through the space with no chaperones in sight.[2]

The former teacher in me was stunned. All museum trips require forethought and planning beyond just logistics. This museum in particular isn't one where students, especially White ones, should roam around with no one to offer them context, ask them questions, and help them connect past with present. (At one point, a group of boys darted in front of me in an exhibit, declared there was nothing in there to look at, then kept going. The space in question included images and a video discussing police brutality and ongoing movements for justice ... as in, the very history they're living through *right now*. I wanted to weep. I also hoped

2   MAGA is a reference to "MAKE AMERICA GREAT AGAIN," a presidential campaign slogan for Donald Trump.

the police group would stop and meditate on it.)

The mom in me was similarly horrified. I've been on enough field trips as both a student and chaperone to know what can go down, and there were so many opportunities for them to both cause trouble and be troubled by others. I would *not* have been okay with my own kids being on a trip managed like this.

I've lived and worked in D.C. for seven years. I see tourists in MAGA hats all the time, milling around Union Station en route to a duck boat tour or whatever, and I've never said a word. Pointed glances? Sure. But I keep it moving (as soon as they stop blocking the escalator, anyway. *Stand right, walk left, people!*). I was planning to keep that streak alive.

But something about these MAGA-hatted kids, after the cop, in This Museum, just gets me. No, not the kids. The (seemingly absent?!) adults. Because behind every MAGA-hatted kid who may or may not know better, there are typically multiple adults who absolutely should.

So, when I finally see a group with a chaperone, I introduce myself and say something. I explain that I used to teach and I'm a mom, so I was surprised to see so many of these kids walking around unsupervised, with no one to contextualize this often-heavy content. And then I ask about the hats.

"You're touring this museum that details excruciating history, and you've got a student with you who is wearing what's frequently considered akin to a present-day Klan hood.…"

(As soon as I say 'Klan,' the red-hatted student flips the cap from his head onto the floor.)

"… I'm not sure he has the knowledge or judgment to fully understand the implications of the choice he's making, which is why I'm talking to you as the adult in this situation. Did you or your colleagues talk to him about that?"

He stammers. "I, uh … I mean, he has the right to wear it . . ."

I'm thinking, *I'm not the government. I'm not a cop, I'm not a public official, and I've in no way suggested that he doesn't have the right to wear this or anything else. Indeed, I happen to believe students have more rights to self-expression than most student dress codes permit. I also happen to have a right to express myself, which I often choose to use when I see things that disturb me.*

I reply, "Yes, he has a right to wear it. I'm asking you if anyone *talked* to him about it, especially before wearing it here. People chant that slogan while committing hate crimes. It's the slogan of a person who authorizes ripping children from their parents' arms and imprisoning them. That hat provokes real fear and terror in people. Has anyone talked to him about what it means to wear something like that and in a place like this?"

He stammers again. "I mean, I happen to agree with you about the president, but I'm not trying to be political…."

I'm not trying to be political. Those words clatter around in my head, sounding worse and worse with every moral conviction they crash into. I completely understand the impulse behind them; for teachers, "being political" is a huge taboo. *But this isn't even political,* I think. *Well, it is, in the same way that everything is political. But what about basic decency, which at a minimum, demands that we **not** silently condone human rights abuses?* What about teaching young people about the broader historical context they inhabit, and what their words, gestures, and actions signal within that context? About understanding the possible consequences of your choices? Why is it "political" to publicly oppose a symbol of the violent family separation that's happening right now, yet it's okay to condemn one a few floors down when discussing similar abuses in a different historical moment? No one is saying tell the kid he should vote Democrat when he gets older. This isn't about partisanship. It's about morality and the mis-education of young people. About the mis-education of so many teachers, too.

I thank him for listening and walk away. By this point, I know I won't be able to appreciate any of this unless I block out as much of the outside world as possible. I download the museum app and head toward the lockers to grab my headphones so I can do a self-guided tour while hearing at least something of the museum itself. As I'm walking back toward the exhibits, I see another crowd of students from this same school, including more boys in MAGA hats amongst a smattering of students of color. The sight of them, and the memory of being young and Black in majority-White spaces, sends a bolt of lightning straight to the pit of my stomach.

My heels turn again, toward the chaperones, both White men. I introduce myself and mention that I spoke to another of their colleagues not long before. I start to ask about the hats, and one of them cuts me off. "YOU DON'T HAVE THE RIGHT TO TELL THEM WHAT TO WEAR! THIS IS A FREE COUNTRY!"

"And I didn't. I'm trying to ask whether anyone has talked to them about what those hats mean. Please don't make assumptions about what you **think** I'm going to say before I have a chance to speak." He moves in closer and says that I'm being rude. I don't budge an inch. *Why yes, suh. I's one uppity Negro.*

At this point his colleague steps in and he walks off. Colleague explains that he understands my "strong feelings" but that they're kids and they don't get it and they just saw it on a souvenir stand or something and he doesn't really know why they got it or who was there or whatever and I don't know him as a parent and he doesn't know me as a parent but surely I can understand they didn't intend anything by it because kids, y'know.

I breathe deep. Some part of me, the part that thinks about things like discriminatory dress codes a lot, wonders whether he'd have the same laissez-faire attitude had a group of girls found some American flag tube tops on that stand and decided to wear those around the museum. *Would their midriffs get the same deference as these boys' racist headgear?* I doubt it, but I don't ask. The actual hats are what's at issue here, not the hypothetical tube tops.

I sigh and smile. "I'm sure they didn't intend any harm; that's why I'm talking to *you*." I mention the unaccompanied students, reiterating how it's our job as adults to help them make sense of things this serious. He agrees I have a point about supervision but repeats the "I dOn'T gEt poLITIcal and tell them what to think" bit.

Sigh. "I'm not asking you to tell them what to think. I'm not even asking you to ask them to take their hats off. I'm asking if anyone talked to them about it. The same way you probably talk to them about how they present themselves online, or in the future for a job interview, there's a conversation to be had here. Especially given what that slogan represents."

What may be lost on young students should at least be apparent to the adults around them. *How does any educated, fair-minded adult **not** feel the extreme dissonance of the "GREAT AGAIN" on their "MAKE AMERICA GREAT AGAIN" hats in a space like this? Which part of this timeline is the "great" part they think we should reclaim? Enslavement? Jim Crow? To say nothing of the very much ongoing state-sanctioned violence against Black and brown people.... Which part of that is GREAT? What part of this history are they hoping becomes real AGAIN?*

Mom me comes back as I keep talking, thinking of how lucky they are to have been approached by offended-but-empathetic me, versus someone far angrier and less interested in a teachable moment. I keep talking. "There are people in D.C. who wouldn't think twice about knocking a hat like that right off of someone's head . . ."

To say nothing of how their classmates of color may feel about it. Of what they're learning about their place in this school community as they watch their White peers buy and wear racist emblems while their teachers say and do **nothing**. *Shouldn't their sense of safety and belonging merit at least a* **conversation**? *A suggestion that someone is even considering that they* **might** *feel differently about this, that their rights and perspectives are as relevant as their White peers. How are they still not clearing a bar* **this** *low?* I have so many questions.

By now first guy is back. He tries to tag back into the conversation asking, "Who are you? Do you work here?" Picking up on my comment about personal presentation, he adds, "And hey, what about how YOU present YOURself? How would YOU like it if somebody said something to you about your tattoos or whatever?!" He makes a sweeping, dismissive gesture that parallels my upper body, from the inky arm hugging my journal to my chest to my locs.

I nearly laugh out loud. *This man has NO clue. As though I, a very Black woman in a racist and sexist society, have never given* **any** *thought to* what other people might think about how I present myself until he said something.

Also? The tattoo in question? It's a bold script on my forearm that reads "Unbought & Unbossed." *Shirley Chisholm's campaign memorabilia is literally hanging in an exhibit only feet above our heads.*

The irony burns but I'm unmoved. "Sir, I'm not talking to you right now, I'm having a conversation with your colleague." I turn back, repeating that students should be better supervised and supported to understand the gravity of this museum's contents and that someone should have a thoughtful conversation with them about those hats. I say, "Thank you for listening," then head out the doors toward the nearest cab.

I call my husband as soon as I can, just to vent to someone I trust. I feel so off-kilter; relieved to have spoken up when something felt wrong but also like I wished I hadn't even gone, much less spoken to anyone. My spouse gets it.

He then reminds me of an Army-ism that's stuck with him for a long time: "When you fail to correct a deficiency, you set a new standard." He mentions the time, a few months ago, when he got kicked out of a casino for calling out a guy wearing Nazi garb. That story crossed my mind the moment I left the museum; it's exactly why I wanted to call him. "It's messed up and you deserve to just get to enjoy the museum like you wanted," he says. "But somebody has to make it uncomfortable to spread hate, especially in a place like that."

I agree. Every day, we see fresh reminders that the White supremacist violence and theft on which this country was built has never ended; it's only occasionally gone (somewhat) underground during moments of progress. Good, fair-minded people outnumber overt bigots, to be sure. But our numbers are irrelevant if we say and do nothing while hateful people re-normalize bigotry—especially among young White boys and men, whose radicalization already has a stark and growing body count.

Someone needs to interrupt the hateful messages they're getting far earlier on, and at a minimum, help kids like these avoid risking their and their classmates' safety by cluelessly trolling the wrong person. I hope their teachers eventually choose to do that work.

In the meantime, I'll just be That Person asking questions, and hoping that whoever needs to ponder them does.

SABRINA JOY STEVENS is a Midatlantic Regional Progressive Education Fellow and a mother, writer, education advocate, and former teacher based in Washington, D.C. She is a founding member of EduColor, a collective that works to elevate the voices of people of color in the education policy dialogue.

Social Action Activity for "Red Hats in the Black Museum"
Focusing on the power of story to change minds

Social action doesn't happen unless we inform others why we are moving to create change. Too many people often believe the surface-level stories and buy into messages such as "climate change is a hoax" or "all lives matter," not yet understanding the science of climate change or the weight of history behind Black Lives Matter.

For this activity, research an issue about which you want to socially affect others. Instead of focusing on statistics, learn about the personal stories of people and places that are affected by the issue.

Next, perhaps you might find ways to amplify the voices of, and stand in solidarity and alliance with, the people whose stories you are learning. Alternatively, craft your own writing or story that uses the personal narratives you've uncovered as evidence to support your position on the issue, being mindful of citing and representing the people of those narratives as powerful, intelligent, capable, and dignified.

Narrative, according to social psychologist Jerome Bruner and other researchers, is the most effective method to teach and learn. Why not use it more often to promote social action?

DEEP DIVE

Wendy Welch

*In this story, Wendy shares what happens when she has audiences
with the "powerful men in suits" who make decisions that impact the
welfare of her community in Appalachia. The power here is in Wendy's
resolution to tell the truth and keep telling it, as well as in her reflection
that small incremental changes in health care coverage happened due to
hers and others' telling of truth. In her own words: "A thousand drops
of water, over time, can carve out a canyon ... or fill it" (All names are
pseudonyms.)*

As the director of a medical organization that builds health infra-
structure, my job is to keep coalfields Appalachia and its "poor, sick,
underserved" inhabitants on the minds of those powerful men in suits
who reside in our state's capital, never letting their policy plans boil down
to "thank God the leak is at the other end of the boat."

I took the job to get health insurance for my husband and me
because it was so hard for us to find as small business owners. (We own
an independent bookstore.) The irony of working in healthcare to get
my family insurance was not lost as I argued and advocated for care and

coverage on behalf of rural citizens throughout the state. Because of this often required networking with state officials, one year I found myself attending the Governor's Summit on Rural Prosperity at an upscale resort.

Yes, that is the mismatch it sounds like. The worst part is, I went anyway. Advocates tend to justify these moments as "see and be seen." My colleague Allele says such summits are a rare opportunity to get small-group time with big names—plus, there's always the chance that they will actually listen to you as you.

Allele is the director of another organization working in the health-economics intersection, her job is statewide compared to my regional. She knows and is respected by pretty much everybody in state government—a good friend to have at conferences and at your back. I let her persuade me.

Besides, when was I ever going to stay at such an expensive resort on my own dime? The posh dark rooms smelt of old money and expensive lotions. Inaugural events at the conference ended with an oyster bar and s'mores roast on the lawn, rewards for a hard day's work listening to people explain why we were doing so much better than we thought, and how it was all going to come out right in the end.

The Governor would address us tomorrow, flanked by members of his cabinet. Allele nudged me. "We know somebody in the cabinet—Bob. He spoke at one of my conferences last year, and he visited your bookstore a while back. Remember?"

Bob had been part of a leadership group visiting my shop almost exactly two years ago to the day. A group of rising business and government leaders wanted to "meet people and ask questions about living in a rural area" and had been given my name by friends who worked in rural health. Sixteen program members, mostly in their twenties and thirties, looked around the store with condescending smiles carefully hidden and asked us about life in the coalfields.

The bookstore café served a mountain fusion lunch of specially spiced pinto beans in Asian tacos, followed by deep-dish pie made from apples picked in our backyard. After dessert and the requisite exclaiming over its excellence, Our Good Chef Karlie told the group her life story. A large woman whose signature uniform is heavy metal black t-shirts, Karlie uses a doo-rag to keep a mane of frizzy hair out of her eyes as she cooks. She favors biking shorts that allow her magnificent tattoos airtime. One leg sports a very accurate likeness of Edgar Allen Poe; the other has the Telltale Heart with a dagger plunged into it, above a raven sitting on a cask of amontillado.

Karlie told Bob's group about the depression that enveloped her following the deaths of her grandmother, mother, marriage, and career in rapid succession, a downward spiral complicated by prescriptions of antidepressants and pain medicines following an accident. You could see them trying to take the narrative at face value and not judge, especially when Karlie said, "They'd take one look at me, and just hand over a drug, like that was all I wanted." Finally, Karlie found a doctor who told her what she needed to hear: too many meds, let's scale back and return you to yourself. Her struggle now, she concluded, was to find affordable coverage for her, her wife Sam—an EMT whose job paid well but not enough to cover adding Karlie to the policy—and their five children.

Karlie's life experiences led to questions that slowly turned the conversation from "what happened" to "why didn't you … ?" By the time they learned that Karlie dropped out of college to seek help for mental health issues, an all-too-familiar thought shift was in high gear, redirecting the group toward a conventional conclusion: blame the victim. Moving from Karlie to the entire region, the group danced around a theme that we'd heard many times before: "Poverty is caused by people who won't get their act together, not the very reason people can't."

It's an old tactic, one we've seen used in various parts of the country. One visitor brought up a recent state-sponsored project, a prominent building on the interstate intended to revitalize the region's art scene. It had produced the opposite effect. The earnest young future leader asked why locals hadn't supported it, as that might have helped it fulfill its mission. "Don't people have to help themselves to a certain extent? Isn't art one of the most accessible ways to do that?" she asked, waving her hands with sincere passion.

The project was a pet peeve of locals, so I dove in with relish, explaining that regional artists had been told it was coming rather than consulted. Local artists were not consulted. Their talents and needs went unacknowledged. While the macro plan—to integrate varied artists into its goal—to collect regional crafts under one roof near the Interstate— seemed to serve the convenience of tourists, nobody considered where that art originated. The plan saved tourists from driving bumpy back roads to explore little towns off the beaten track. Statewide tourism would increase.

Perhaps you see why the residents of said little towns might not like this idea?

I'd barely begun warming to what an ill-informed, poorly conceived approach this tax-based collectivization was when the leader of the group leapt to her feet. "We never introduced ourselves at the beginning," she said, interrupting mid-word. "Let's go around and do that now."

Lawyers, policy makers, academics: names and titles ran together until we got to Bob, who gave me a big smile and said he ran the state department that authorized and funded the project I'd been dissing. People were looking at the floor, out the window, at Karlie's tattoos—anywhere but at Bob and me.

With what shreds of dignity remained, I thanked them all for coming and suggested we take a walk. As we headed toward the coolness of the town's Creekside Greenbelt (a paved walking path) in the blazing afternoon sun, I saw Bob making for me at a fast clip, sweating in his tailored suit.

The leader of the group had been walking at my side, chatting; when she saw Bob bearing down on us, she offered a sympathetic look. "Bob really is a good guy. He wants to make things better," she said—and then moved ahead, trapping me neatly next to the good guy.

Bob held out a business card with one hand, wiping sweat from his eyes with the other. "I would like to talk to you."

My response may not have been polite, but it came from honesty: "Well, I don't want to talk to you. If I'd known who you were, I would never have said anything."

He grinned. "Yeah, I gathered as much. C'mon, look at it from my perspective. All I get are reports about how great it's going. I'm surrounded by yes men all day. You're the first person to tear it down in front of me. Tell me what people are saying."

What people were saying could be summed up in a two-word phrase starting with F, but this felt like my last chance to prove I could be polite. Bob listened carefully as I outlined the concerns artists often expressed and he thanked me. Then, as we closed the circle on the Green-belt, Bob explained in quick, concise terms that the reasons for the project's failure were known to its creators. They planned to do nothing, for political reasons, which he outlined. He wanted me to understand that his hands were tied, but he was most appreciative of my candor and believed I deserved the same.

I should probably have been pleased a politician was talking to me with such confidence. Perhaps Bob meant to signal the beginning of a beautiful professional mutual usefulness. Yet I only felt fury at being trapped into opening up to someone whose response was "what can I do about it" with a shrug rather than a question mark. Someone who knew that response going into the conversation he chased me down to have. I also felt guilty because Bob did seem like the nice guy he so clearly wanted me to see. If a career politician couldn't fix this broken thing, did that make him the enemy?

Fast forward two years and a day. See me sitting beside Allele at the Governor's Summit for Rural Prosperity the morning after we'd enjoyed the oysters, listening to a senator talk about the great strides made toward affordable healthcare in our state. He informed us, with the energy of a ringmaster building suspense, that the governor and his cabinet would be arriving shortly. The room had already begun to fill with bodyguards.

We were instructed to get excited. Allele reminded me again how Bob had visited my bookstore once, hadn't he, with that group of young leaders? She had no idea how well I remembered. I'd never told anyone the story.

Just then my phone dinged. Our Good Chef Karlie, as we call her, sent a simple message:

> We just got a phone call. Our health insurance has been mishandled for the last six months. They are making us pay back a thousand dollars and canceling the insurance because Sam can get covered at work. We can't afford to add me to hers, but that doesn't factor in. Since it's available, we have to take it.

Sam and Karlie married the year before, as much so they could benefit from insurance and tax breaks as to cement a loving relationship that had finally become legal in all fifty states. Now the wedding would break up the insurance discounts?

Karlie was asking me, as someone who "knew a lot about health stuff," to help. The problem was, I knew exactly what was wrong, and it was unfixable. They'd fallen into something known as the Family Glitch, a flaw in the Affordable Care Act that didn't account for the number of family members versus salary and thus amortize who could afford to pay what. It was a horrible flaw, and it had caught thousands of family breadwinners in its crevices. Worse, state governments were trying to claw back the money they felt had been "lost" by misinformation about the Family Glitch. More terrible than getting no help at all is to believe you had coverage, only to be hit with a huge bill for "repayment of services" six months or a year later.

I messaged back, explaining what was happening, but without any ability to suggest practical steps they could take to avoid the fine or loss of coverage. In fact, it felt a lot like the way Bob had handled our conversation two years before: "Here's what's wrong and here's why. And I'm so sorry I can't fix it."

No, Karlie and Sam, the hardest-working couple I knew, were well and truly stuck. That was the moment when the speaker who'd instructed us to get excited said, "We would have brought the governor in by plane at the private airfield, but we had to sell the state jet last year before the auditors came."

I am not a naïve person. We've all been there, that place where you feel so overwhelmed you can't think, can't hear, can't swallow. Your throat forgets how to function and the stone in your stomach feels like it's going to rip through your guts and fall on the floor. It's not a good place, nor a productive one. That was the moment the doors opened and the governor—surrounded by his cabinet, including the newly promoted Bob—walked in. And out of that miasma of unfiltered purple fury, no thought, no plan, I said, out loud, "Fuck you, you bastard." And burst into tears.

The room had been laughing and starting to applaud the entering cabinet, so only those nearest noticed my outburst. Allele grabbed my arm and shoved me upwards, out of my seat, and toward the door. "Go," she hissed, pushing me headfirst into the stomach of a bodyguard. The guard, taking one look at Allele's stone-rigid face, held the door for me. I walked right past Bob, who adjusted his shoulders a little higher when he saw me, snapping his eyes straight ahead.

Outside, as I walked up and down the garden paths, a modicum of control returned. Or maybe I admitted there was no such thing. There was no way to assist anyone trapped the way Karlie was. These men in suits would swear they were happy to listen, but they wouldn't make any changes if I told them what was happening to people like Karlie. They already knew, these people like Bob, "a genuinely nice guy" who couldn't make a difference, or worse, wouldn't.

They didn't want to make waves at any expense to themselves. And they knew that rocking the boat would serve no long-term good, that one action could be hidden inside the other. The line between *can't* and *won't* is tiny in some circumstances, the distinction between power and willingness blurry. Was I holding Bob accountable for refusing to get involved, yet absolving myself? Why was I at this expensive inn listening to stupid classist jokes if I couldn't tell Karlie's story to any effect?

People in power don't have simple choices, I could see that. But they do have influence, a lot more than most people. Whether any of us were using it or not, only we knew. Good guy, bad guy, nobody's guy, who could say? But here I sat—or, in that moment, walked—in circles among the manicured lawns and flower beds, doing no good and crying because of it. Who could I help? See and be seen, my arse. Maybe there wasn't a way to do better in these circles complicated by power. Justification? Reality? Absolution?

I knew that I wanted *now* what Bob had wanted *then*, that hot day on the Greenbelt: to feel like a good guy. But sometimes, being a good guy wasn't enough. There was nothing I could do to get healthcare coverage for two of the best people in Appalachia. All I had in my hand to fight with was the truth of their tale, and it wouldn't be enough. Nor would that dramatic, childish f-bomb flung by impotent rage move anyone. I was useless at this political game.

The story would end there if it weren't for the swimming pool.

That evening, after I'd regained a little adult equilibrium, I followed Allele to the S'more pit because chocolate and despair are a natural pairing. Below us, something that looked like water sparkled in the moonlight. Glancing over the cliff, I beheld a large swimming pool, beautifully lit with purple sconces, lying empty some seventy feet below.

"Thought the pool was closed. Brochure said so," I observed to no one in particular.

Another S'more maker looked up. "Oh no, we were in it this afternoon. Air's a bit brisk, but when the sun's out, it's just about warm enough. You could go tomorrow during the break."

Allele drew in a breath. Knowing me well, Allele anticipated what hadn't bubbled to the surface in my own thoughts yet. "First of all, it's not heated. Secondly, there's no lifeguard, plus it's dark," she said, as if to no one in particular.

I'm a strong swimmer who, since childhood, has indulged in this solitary sport as much for joy as exercise. Because my job involved so much travel, I usually took my exercise bobbing about in little hotel pools only four feet deep, treading water rather than swimming laps. Since we often work in partnership, Allele knew my cardinal rule about hotels: *must have pool, no matter how small.* In fact, for years I slipped into pool after pool at hotels across Appalachia, believing I was swimming, never realizing I was only treading water—until the day of reckoning came.

What Allele didn't know—what no one knew, because I was too ashamed to speak of it—was that one day out of the blue (no pun intended) I stuck my face into a big fancy hotel pool of regulation lap length, preparatory to performing the long, elegant strokes that form the water dance called Freestyle ...

... and had a panic attack.

My therapist friend Cami says most people start coping with their own mortality around midlife; death hoving into view on the horizon makes us hyperaware of even nominal danger. The insidious part is that while we're developing these fears about all the ways we could die, we start avoiding activities we like, eventually winding up a joyless corpse long before we lie down for the last time—a thousand little deaths in exchange for one big one. We forget how to swim because treading water is safer.

Death by drowning didn't sound so bad that night. Weren't we all dead already, living this crazy existence of pretending that what we did mattered, that we could help each other when it counted, that it was important to attend conferences and try to change people's minds about things like access to care? I was going to die, we all would, maybe those without healthcare sooner than the rest, so if tonight was the night, who cared?

Please understand, I don't mean I felt suicidal. Rather, it felt as though despair had rendered me invincible. Someone with nothing to lose will risk nothing to gain something back. I gave my S'more to Allele and went back to get my suit. She shrugged and stuck to the fire pit.

I took a long running leap. My skin felt everything, more alive than any part of me had been all day: the breezy softness of cool air against my shoulders; grit on the stones around the pool beneath my bare feet; the breath-stealing enclosure of cold water racing up my body, purple darkness above, blue light below. I could feel my heart beating. I could hear blood singing in my ears. I couldn't breathe, but it didn't matter because I was in charge.

Up through the water, into the air, sucking in sweet still coldness, plunging back down. Glorious it became, to play in the water that night under those cold, impersonal stars. Fear could go drown itself; if I were already living the life of a dead person, time to make the most of it. Face-first, breathing in the three-stroke style of a long-distance swimmer, the laps sped by, one after another. How could dying be worse than those thousand little deaths of realizing how powerless we all are, to be the change we wish to see in the world? Consign that platitude to the bottom of the inky black ocean where it belonged.

Swimming is some of the best Zen time you'll ever get; there's nothing to do but think and calculate laps. I get that water could be seen as a tired metaphor for fighting a thing that doesn't care about you one way or another—not that any of us know any forces like that in the U.S. Government or anywhere else, of course. All I'm saying is that despair can make you die inside, or it can make you stronger. I don't know why or how I got zapped with the live end of despair's healing properties, I didn't care. As I ignored my thoughts by concentrating on arm strokes and counting, things began to sort themselves inside my head.

It is as hard to be angry in the water as to be angry at it. Perhaps elementals do something to humans, pulling away from us the things we bring into them; maybe that's what God designed earth, air, water, and fire to do. Like its sister elementals, water doesn't care what we think about it or what we want from it. We can be angry and lash out; we can be tired and float; it does not make a difference to the water.

As water and air ebbed and flowed, I didn't so much convince myself that telling Sam and Karlie's story would help as that it was necessary. Telling the stories to people in suits who might shrug, might smile, might placate, but also might listen—this was my only weapon. And I knew how to tell stories, just as I knew how to swim in deep water.

So I wrote it up, and it still floats between air and water, doing its work. And here am I, a survivor of strange undercurrents in unfathomable places. I've told Karlie and Sam's story to many politicians and pontificates, as others have told stories of their loved ones trapped in those whirlpools that never want to let you out.

It is true that those of us telling people's stories over and over eventually do see shrugs and smiles become movement of a more definite nature. Slowly, steadily, over the last five years, a tweak in numbers here—they dropped the repayment requirement clause in my state within six months of the Summit—a change in the wording there—"for heads of household, see Appendix One"—and the Glitch has been whittled down to nothing. Other bad things have gone away. A few good things have come. Never without a fight. And never without the stories of those worth fighting for.

A thousand drops of water, over time, can carve out a canyon.

Or fill it.

WENDY WELCH is executive director of the Graduate Medical Education Consortium of Southwest Virginia. She is also the author of *The Little Bookstore Of Big Stone Gap* and *Fall Or Fly* (detailing how the substance abuse crisis crashed rural foster care systems). Her first work of fiction is *Bad Boy in the Bookstore*. She also is the editor of two anthologies: *Public Health In Appalachia* and *From the Front Lines of the Appalachian Addiction Crisis: Healthcare Providers Discuss Opioids, Meth and Recovery*. A lifelong advocate for coalfields Appalachia, Wendy divides her time between enjoying its natural beauty and cultural offerings and working to make it a more just and vibrant place.

Social Action Story Activity for "Deep Dive"
Reframing the short- and long-term

Wendy's story brings us back to one of Val Brown's essential questions for activists: *How do I define short-term and long-term success?*

One of the most important gifts we can give ourselves, as well as the people we work with and for, is reflection on our own definitions and experiences of what we would consider short- and long-term success. For Wendy, long-term success in advocating for humane health care doesn't come with straightforward steps to a triumphant outcome. Instead, the road was frustrating, and the change happened slowly, thanks to tireless efforts.

Spend some time journaling or in conversation to reflect on the long-term successes in your life and/or communities. The achievements you consider could be personal, professional, or activism-related. What short-term successes or failures lined the path for you or the communities involved?

We also owe it to ourselves to seek out stories like Wendy's, of how action over the long-term has led to success—especially when our current short-term might feel exhausting or fruitless. Stories of people resisting injustice have much to teach us about our work in the here and now.

IN THE CLOSET

Anne Schwartz

At a tradition-steeped, all-girls boarding school whose claimed mission is to help each student find their true self, what happens when that self isn't a girl? Anne reminds us that, although many social action stories are about great success or creating change, sometimes we must seek out different spaces to grow as change-makers.

I GOT YELLED AT IN A CLOSET.

The irony is not lost on me. I was in a closet, being yelled at because I, a not-so-subtle not-so-tactful straight white twenty-seven-year-old woman, was aggressively rude to my boss in an all-staff meeting about extra students in our school.

Here's the thing about working at an all-girls school: sometimes there are boys. Sometimes students come as girls and then tell you that was never actually their truth. Sometimes they figure it out while at school. A boarding school that was designed to help girls find themselves sometimes really helps them find themselves.

Sometimes that self is not a girl.

It started with pants. At this school, the girls wore white dresses for graduation and, while there is a whole bucket of patriarchy in that alone, the school didn't know what to do when one of our seniors wanted to wear a white suit. When I say "the school didn't know," I mean the Head of School and the Dean of Students. Most of the faculty fell on the side of "let the child wear pants," which is luckily where we ended up.

From pants, we went to pronouns. In 2013, I didn't know much about people who were trans or their experiences. The women's colleges were just starting to come up with plans. But I was in a small town in upstate New York. What I knew about people was that you should call them what they ask to be called, refer to them how they want to be referred, and changing their presentation shouldn't change how much you love them.

There was a lot of fear swirling around the school, mostly from the older faculty. I heard things like, "How do these children know they are boys?" "What if they just waited until they left here and then became boys?" "What if girls didn't want to room with boys?" "What if they changed their minds?" "What if we are harming them by letting them do this?"

So, when the Head of School called a staff meeting and said, "We do not have boys here. The girls may pick their names, but they will all have female pronouns. We are a girls' school," I yelled from the back, "But we do have boys! At least two. They told us."

The room got quiet. This was not the way you spoke to our Head. This was not the way one behaved in a 200-year-old school steeped in tradition. After the meeting, the Head pulled me aside and dragged me into the mail room closet. "You do not change minds by yelling, and mine is made up. This is done," she said and stormed out. It was the only time in my three years there that I saw her lose her carefully constructed civility.

I wish this was a story of triumph. I mean, in some ways, it is. The boys in that class just graduated college as good men with no one even suggesting they wear dresses under the ugly polyester robes. They found colleges that allowed them to be their most authentic selves.

I left the school that year after twice being told my values didn't align with the school's. They didn't, and I wasn't willing to argue about it in a closet.

———————————————————

ANNE SCHWARTZ is a secondary math teacher dedicated to intersectional feminism, anti-racist teaching, and restorative justice. She lives in southern California with her two cats and enjoys rock climbing and sewing. She is currently working on her doctorate in educational leadership with a focus on Whiteness in teaching.

Social Action Activity for "In the Closet"
The Power of How to Walk Away

In this activity, you'll leverage a question Val Brown asked us to consider in her forward: *How do I walk away when it is time?*

Jeannie Lythcott, one of Kirstin's mentors, once told a group of teacher candidates that an important aspect of a successful and meaningful career in education was finding a new school when the work became too hard—and that an equally important aspect of success was finding a new school when the work became too *easy*.

We walk away from important work for all kinds of reasons. Sometimes, it's because other opportunities present themselves. Sometimes, it's because other people can bring *their* insights, skills, and dispositions to the work. But sometimes, particularly in social activism work, we might step back or away for reasons that involve strong feelings of uncertainty, frustration, anger, or pain.

As Val's forward reminds us, "the work of social action is incredibly messy, and you should know that anyone who decides to act will accrue bumps and bruises. Movement, by definition, requires opening yourself up to risk." How can we make peace with the bumpiness and messiness of social action, especially if we believe it is time for us to walk away?

Anne's story shows us one way forward: find ways to act and speak within your integrity. If you develop an ongoing reflection practice (whether through writing, drawing, or in conversation with others) as part of your social action work, you'll also develop inner guideposts about what your boundaries are. For many of us, those boundaries shift as we develop new skills, practice negotiating productive conflict and criticism, and widen our understandings of the work.

But sometimes, if you can't determine a way to stay within your integrity, it's time to walk away. If you find yourself in such a situation, remember to give yourself grace and patience. Consider celebrating by listing, as Val does in the forward, the good of what happened during, or as a result of your participation. It might also be useful to remember that such an experience might be galvanizing for you, as in Anne's story.

Anne's story also reminds us that all of us can work to renormalize how gender is experienced, described, and respected:

- Add the pronouns you go by to your social media profiles, your email signature, and your business cards. This is particularly important if you are cisgender because it normalizes the practice for those of us whose pronouns may be unexpected or in flux.

- Don't assume someone's pronouns. Ask if you're not sure: "What pronouns do you go by?" Instead of describing "that lady" to your toddler at the grocery store, use "that person."

- When you meet someone for the first time, give the pronouns you go by and ask your new acquaintance what pronouns they go by.

- If you plan an event or oversee a workplace with name tags, provide structures and encouragement for participants and employees to publicly share their pronouns.

If someone (particularly a student) tells you their pronouns, but those pronouns differ from what you hear other people using, speak to that person privately about who knows and who you can tell.

CRIC? CRAC!

SHERRY NORFOLK AND LYN FORD

*In this story, three librarians do the necessary work to teach a
culturally responsive lesson to elementary school students in Miami,
whose schools included many Haitian refugee children. These librarians
researched the storytelling traditions of Haiti and chose stories that would
promote similarities across differences, to address the tension and unrest
that schools were experiencing. Sherry and Lyn show us how intentionality
and time devoted to creating an inclusive space for Haitian young people
"open[ed] windows—just a crack—enough for acceptance and understanding to seep in."*

IN 1985, WHEN THE HAITIAN BOAT LIFT BROUGHT THOUSANDS of Haitian
refugees into southern Florida, Sherry was a children's librarian with the
Miami-Dade Public Library. Suddenly, the schools in North Miami were
flooded with children who spoke "differently," dressed "differently," and
acted and reacted "differently" than their fellow students.

The result was predictable: immediate resistance, distrust, and unrest
in school populations. As one school official explained, "The Haitian kids
are being metaphorically kicked to the bottom rung of society. They are

being stepped on to keep them in their place."

When its new building opened in 1975, the North Dade Regional Library where Sherry worked had begun storytelling outreach to local schools. By 1985, the schools had become convinced of the value of storytelling. It was no surprise when the library began to receive calls from desperate principals, counselors, media specialists, and teachers. The callers asked if the storytellers might use the power of story to change the viewpoints of those who considered themselves "the Americans," so that they no longer saw their new classmates as "strangers" or "other."

The three children's librarians/storytellers accepted the challenge and got to work. Luckily, Diane Wolkstein had published her beautifully-researched book, *The Magic Orange Tree and Other Haitian Folktales* (Knopf) in 1978. So, the storytellers had easy access to an excellent source of stories. The book included important information about the traditional way these stories were told in Haiti, and their cultural significance. Each teller developed a small-but-mighty repertoire of Haitian tales and set forth.

In nearly all of the 25 elementary schools and ten middle schools where the stories were told, the experiences were the same:

"Cric?" the storytellers always began. The "American" kids quizzically stared, and the Haitian kids lit up and whispered, "Crac!"

The "American" kids' heads whipped around to see who had said that.

The call was repeated: "Cric?" "Crac!" (A little louder this time.)

Then the storyteller explained that she was going to tell stories from the island of Haiti.

"How many of you are from Haiti?" Hesitant hands went up.

"Then you may know some of these stories!" Hopeful eyes, tiny nods—they might know one of the stories, and they would definitely welcome a familiar tale.

"In Haiti, as your new friends know, storytelling is very important, and there are certain rules that must be followed. For example, a story-teller must ask permission of the audience to tell a story by asking 'Cric?' If the audience wants to hear the story, they answer, 'Crac!' So ... 'Cric?'"

"CRAC!"

And the stories began. Sometimes funny, sometimes a bit scary, always fascinating, the stories captivated the entire audience, weaving an invisible but tangible web among the children.

At the conclusion of each assembly, the storytellers reminded the listeners that these stories were from Haiti, the homeland of their new classmates and that those same children probably knew lots more stories to tell.

"Ask them!" the librarians urged, giving children a couple of minutes to locate and query a Haitian classmate. They saw lots of happy nods and delighted grins throughout the audience.

"We all know stories to tell each other," the librarian/storytellers finished. "You just learned that we all like the same kinds of stories. We get scared by the same things, excited about the same things, and laugh about the same things. We're more alike than different. So, listen to each other's stories—and come to the library for more!"

Did those forty-five-minute performances work miracles? Maybe not. But they opened windows—just a crack—enough for acceptance and understanding to seep in. Principals and teachers reported that the tension in the schools lessened after that. Children, they reported, had begun to treat each other with more respect than fear. The stories went beyond the opening of windows through which to see and hear. They opened doors to invite children into one another's minds and hearts.

Folktales have the power to break down barriers. They have the power to nurture transformation. They have the power to encourage healing. The power is inherent in the stories, *even when told by people of other cultures*—but only if those tellers do their homework!

All three of those librarians/tellers were Anglo women, none of whom had ever been to Haiti or had Haitian ancestors. But all three did their homework, wanting to present the stories with respect, perception, and authenticity. They studied the rich background material provided by Wolkstein, who *had* been to Haiti to research the stories and the culture and traditions surrounding them. They did their best to share the joy, cleverness, and courage of those tales.

Please note: The tellers did not try to use a Haitian accent. They did not dress in costume. There was no attempt to pretend to be something they were not. And if the librarians/tellers had known a teller who could bring the tales from personal immersion in the Hatian cultural heritage, that teller would have been welcomed to tell.

What the librarian/storytellers did was watch the faces of the Haitian children, whose joy in hearing the familiar tales shone through. Their nods and smiles told the storytellers everything they needed to know: the stories took those children home again and encouraged other children to welcome them to their new home.

That is the education our children desperately need.

SHERRY NORFOLK is an award-winning storyteller, author, and teaching artist who performs and presents nationally and internationally. As a Kennedy Center National Teaching Artist, Wolf Trap Teaching

Artist, Young Audiences Teaching Artist, and Adjunct Professor at Lesley University, Sherry is a recognized leader in arts integration.

LYNETTE (LYN) FORD is a fourth-generation storyteller and Ohio teaching artist. She is the co-author, with storyteller Sherry Norfolk, of *Speak Peace: Words of Wisdom, Work and Wonder* (Parkhurst Brothers) published for the 2019 International Day of Peace.

Social Action Activity for "Cric? Crac!"
The Playfulness of Storytelling Events

Lyn and Sherry's story shows us that, with care to create appropriate safeguards against cultural appropriation, story can be a playful way to celebrate difference, nudge audiences, and sow seeds of change.

Although this story centers on a tale told to audiences of children, it's important to remember that story can serve adults in the same ways. Storytelling can be an invitation for grown-up activists and activist communities to pause, laugh, wonder, and dream together.

Activism is often serious work. Much is on the line, time seems of the essence, and setbacks hurt. We are often navigating frustration, anger, and fear. But these emotions, without respite, lead to tension within organizations and burnout of individuals from causes that need them.

What to do? One way forward is to find ways to build playfulness into your work, and storytelling events can be a great way to do so.

Consider holding a story circle event. You could do this with colleagues at work, students in your class, family members, folks in your faith or activism community, or friends.

In-person is lovely, but we've had great success hosting story events through web conferencing platforms, too. (If you are using a video-conferencing tool, be sure to encourage participants to select a "gallery" view rather than a view that primarily features the speaker.)

Create a welcoming invitation for people to share a story or just attend to listen to others. Draw on your relationships with others to make sure a few people will be willing to share, so you can be sure of having some stories! In our experience, others will feel safe sharing after others have done so. Consider sharing first yourself to assume the most risk.

Don't record or live-stream your event and, if you are together in person, ask that all electronics be turned off and put away for the event. Keeping the event electronics-free helps it feel low-stakes, so people feel safe sharing their stories.

Invite all sorts of stories! Laughter is a wonderful outcome, but sighs, tears, and aching hearts are okay, too.

After each storyteller, allow the group to snap or clap but don't invite discussion. This event is about listening and not responding.

Hosting an event like this allows us to see new sides of people we work closely with and might think we know well. We are often surprised by the person that emerges through a story. An event like this can build community and foster connection and belonging in a group.

ALEJANDRA'S POWER

ALEJANDRA IVANOVICH AND JENNIFER RUDICK ZUNIKOFF

Rhetoric and policy against immigrants impact the safety of more than just its intended targets. In this story, Alejandra fiercely advocates for fundamental human rights of those in her community. This she does even when standing in a place of insecurity herself, a US citizen who immigrated from Venezuela in 2000. Jennifer encourages Alejandra to share her own story in the process, uncovering the power she has to impact the wellbeing of others.

JENNIFER: AS A STORYTELLING COACH, I LISTEN TO A LOT OF STORIES, and I invite each person to listen to her own story from the inside. I believe that no one is more fit to tell a story than the person who has lived it and who has listened to that story from inside herself.

However, sometimes a person cannot tell her own story. Perhaps the storyteller does not speak the language of her audience. Or maybe she does not feel safe sharing her story with the people who most need to hear it. It could be that the storyteller does not even know that she possesses a story to tell.

When it comes to undocumented immigrants, often all of these circumstances are true.

Alejandra Ivanovich is not an undocumented immigrant. She is a U.S. citizen who moved here at the age of thirteen in 1998. Until recently, she felt safe in the United States. She speaks both Spanish and English fluently.

Alejandra is an advocate for undocumented immigrants. She listens to people who have stories to tell. People seek her out because they need someone to understand their stories. Alejandra understands.

Alejandra was born in Caracas, Venezuela. Her mother came from a long line of Italian Catholics. Alejandra's mother's mother moved from Italy to Venezuela with her parents and siblings after World War II.

Alejandra's father's father was a Serbian Jew. Her father's mother was a German Jew. Her grandparents together fled to Venezuela during World War II.

And then there was unrest in her generation. When Alejandra was twelve, one year before Hugo Chavez staged the coup that led to his presidency, a bomb exploded near her mother's office. Her parents decided that Venezuela was no longer safe. Within a year, the family was living in the United States.

Alejandra became a permanent resident of the U.S. in 2000. It wasn't until 2016, when Donald Trump was elected president, that Alejandra felt unsafe living here with only her permanent residency status to protect her. She began the process of becoming a U.S. citizen.

ALEJANDRA: When Donald Trump took office, I was not yet a citizen. I was a permanent resident. I was worried that he would change the laws and have all permanent residents kicked out too. I have my children, and I have a business. I didn't want to get kicked out of my country.

I have lived here for twenty-three years.

———

JENNIFER: I met Alejandra one week before we were each scheduled to speak at the Baltimore County Lights of Liberty protest in July 2019. The Baltimore County protest was one of more than 700 around the world. Most included a vigil to end human detention camps.

I was preparing to speak as a poet and storyteller and as the director of a small organization, The Golden Door: Storytelling for Social Justice. Alejandra was planning to tell the story of an undocumented woman from Guatemala.

Over the phone, she and I had our first conversation about sharing these stories. I asked her, "At the protest, will you be telling some of your own stories?"

At first, Alejandra did not think her personal story was important to tell at the event. She said that the purpose of the protest was to support the undocumented immigrants, and she was a citizen.

Yes, I explained to her, but it is you who are giving a voice here to the stories of undocumented people.

"You are part of their story. And we need to hear your story, too," I said.

Alejandra is modest, but she agreed to tell a piece of her own story at the Lights of Liberty event.

———

Here is the story Alejandra shared with more than 200 people at the protest:

ALEJANDRA: During the (U.S.) presidential election, I had a friend Noelia who had moved to the U.S. from Guatemala. She was concerned about who was going to be our president. "My husband said that if Trump wins, we are going to have to go back to Guatemala," Noelia said.

She told me that she didn't want to return to her country because her life was horrible there. I told her: "Don't worry. According to the polls, Hillary is going to win."

Noelia said to me, "I'm going to turn everything off, and tomorrow morning, let me know who won." She didn't want the stress of watching the TV or listening to the radio during the election.

The night of the election, I was watching the election on television with a friend. When Trump won Florida, I knew we had lost.

I was crying the whole way home. I couldn't sleep that night.

Noelia called at five in the morning. She said, "Who won?"

I said, "I'm sorry, honey. Trump won."

Noelia started crying. Her son was in the background, saying, "I don't want to go to Guatemala! I don't want to go to Guatemala!"

I told her: "Don't worry, honey, I'm going to have a town hall meeting. And we are going to find out what a Trump presidency will be like for all of us."

On the day of the town hall, over 200 people showed up, plus seven local organizations that work with immigrants. I wanted to inform the undocumented people in attendance about what they can do to protect themselves here in America.

I stepped out into the hall during the town hall meeting. I saw a woman in her mid-30s with a special needs son. The woman was intensely crying.

I said, "Are you okay?"

She said, "No, I'm not. My aunt told me you could maybe help me. I have cysts on my ovaries, and they can burst. I need surgery."

I told her, "I'm not a doctor, but give me your phone number, and I'll call you tomorrow." I hugged her for a long time. We held each other.

Over the next month, I took her to several hospitals. They wouldn't take her because she had no insurance. I took her to the ER at a Baltimore hospital. They said there was nothing they could do because she did not have insurance.

I took her to the charge nurse, and I said, "If you don't treat her, I will sue you for negligence." Later that day, I was in my car in the hospital parking lot, shaking because I had made that threat.

Three or four days later, I got a call from a doctor, and we came back on a night the doctor was working. She tested my new friend and said she needed an emergency surgery.

A few months later, I received a phone call from a potential customer for my cleaning business.

She wanted a quote.

When I arrived at her house, I said, "Hi! I am Alejandra Ivanovich, but you can call me Ally."

She said, "Your name is Alejandra Ivanovich? Have you been to _____ hospital recently?"

I thought about the situation and how I was raising hell when I was at the hospital, and I thought, "This is not going to go well with getting my quote."

"Alejandra, I was one of the nurses who assisted during your friend's surgery, and she almost went septic." This woman looked at me. "I want you to know that you saved her life."

When she said that, that's when I understood my power.

You have power, too.

ALEJANDRA IVANOVICH, originally from Venezuela, is a mother of three amazing children and a small business owner who is also pursuing a bachelor's in political science. Alejandra is a community activist for Latinx people, women, and children; she currently serves on the board of Amigos of Baltimore County and the community engagement subcommittee of Census Complete Count.

JENNIFER RUDICK ZUNIKOFF is a storyteller, poet, educator, facilitator, and coach. She is the founder and director of The Golden Door: Storytelling for Social Justice, an organization that brings storytellers and facilitators to schools to coach teachers, educate students, and build safe, encouraging classroom communities. Jennifer was named a 2016 Baltimore Social Innovator by the Warnock Foundation.

Social Action Activity for "Alejandra's Power"
Reflecting on personal power

It is a gift to people and movements when we, like Alejandra and Jennifer, help others understand that their own stories have meaning, value, and power.

For this activity, you might brainstorm a list of possible ways to celebrate and encourage others' stories and experiences. Sometimes it can be as easy as encouraging those dear to us in simple ways to remember that their experiences and their stories, have helped to forge what we love about them.

But this stance has tremendous power at scale, too. How can you use your connections, gifts, and interests to help others value and share stories? How can you work to help create spaces where learning is valued over speed, where missteps have much to celebrate? In your role as a family member, professional, organizer, or simply as someone invested in an issue or a community, what are possible ways you could help others share stories to build identity, change hearts and minds, disrupt, or resist?

It's crucial for us, too, to unpack experiences where we realize we hold power. Growing familiar with the negative potential of power over other people (particularly those of historically oppressed identities or backgrounds), as you did after reading Ursula's story, is an essential way forward to growing as an activist. However, Jennifer and Alejandra show us that reflecting on times when you experienced power for change in a way that positively impacted others is an equally generative practice.

Reflect in writing or in conversation on a time when you felt powerful in a healthy, positive way and were able to help to make a change, as Alejandra does in her story. Describe the situation in some detail. What was it about the experience that helped you realize you held power? What can you use from your reflection in your current context? How can you shift the power you have over others to becoming power you share *with* others?

IDENTITY: HOW WE SHOW UP AND ARE CHANGED BY THE WORK

IN THIS SECTION, WE HEAR STORIES AT THE INTERSECTION OF ACTIVISM and identity. While identity is central to many of the stories in this collection, these stories explicitly explore how our own identities grow and change from the actions we take and how our identities can power the work we do for ourselves and others.

BATHROOMS FOR ALL

Kit Golan

*How do our actions grow as we uncover, learn more about, or lean
into our identities? For Kit, advocating for all-gender restrooms in professional spaces provided opportunities to develop his skills as an activist and
uncover the power of letting more people in his life know an important part
of who he is.*

By the end of my freshman year in college, I was identifying as
trans and using he/him pronouns in some spaces, but I wasn't consistently passing as male. I transferred colleges and found myself in a very
weird space with regard to my gender: I knew I was trans and used he/
him pronouns with my close friends and in queer spaces, but I wasn't out
to my family, and I wasn't even out to the professors on my new campus.

Bathrooms were an especially frustrating experience that year
because my new college had so many single-use bathrooms with gendered
signs on them. These are the bathrooms that are just one small room with
one toilet and a locking door. Selecting the bathroom I should use in a
given situation, based on where I was, who I was with, and who might
be nearby, was excruciating. During Saturday morning brunches with my

friends, we started discussing the state of bathrooms on campus. I pointed out how weird it was that my previous campus, an engineering school in Massachusetts, had more single-use all-gender options than my current school.

My friends and I decided to document the bathrooms in every on-campus building to see where single-use bathrooms were unnecessarily gendered. We wrote a formal proposal to the student life committee, asking that all single-use bathrooms immediately be made all-gender. In re-reading our proposal ten years later, I was amused to note that we managed to describe non-binary people in about ten words (the term "non-binary" wasn't in use yet!), and the types of signs we wanted didn't seem to exist yet either. Most "gender-neutral" bathrooms at the time just had both men and women stick figures on them, which both excluded people who were non-binary and implied that men and women had to look like those two distinct stick figures.

Two buildings on campus provided only multi-stall bathrooms, and we proposed that those buildings have at least one set of bathrooms designated as all-gender. We were doubtful that this request would receive approval, so we were surprised when the committee had us talk to the science department and the library staff and elated when the bathrooms in the basement of the library and the second floor of the science center became gender-neutral.

The process of simultaneously fighting for gender-neutral bathrooms on campus while publicly transitioning was exhausting. I constantly had to defend my claim to manhood: to my family, professors, and even some of my classmates. It felt like the only way I could do that was to conform to every expectation society put on me as a man. By the end of college, I was burnt out on defending my identity and searching for alternatives. After starting testosterone and having top surgery, the idea of not having to fight that battle daily seemed appealing, especially because, as a first-year teacher, there were plenty of other battles I needed to fight! So, I decided to stay in the closet at my first school (and in the Math for America program).

After six years of teaching without talking about my own trans-ness, it became clear my middle schoolers were more trans-aware than I had realized. One transitioned—and they and their friends didn't even know I was trans! The following year, at a gender and sexuality alliance (GSA) meeting, another asked me if I was trans because he had heard rumors that I was. This made me realize that by not addressing my trans-ness outright, I was unintentionally sending the message that being trans-gender was something taboo, something not to discuss, and perhaps even something to be ashamed of.

I realized I needed to come out to my students—so the ones who were trans and gender non-conforming could have a visible role model of an adult who was like them, but also so that my cisgender students wouldn't grow up to be adults thinking they'd never met a trans person because no one "looked like" the trans women they saw in the media.

I wound up coming out twice that year: first to my classes during a special lesson I created for the GLSEN Day of Silence, and then to the whole school, on stage, during the annual GSA assembly. I shared the differences between gender identity, gender expression, and sex assigned at birth. I explained the distinctions between cisgender people (people whose gender identities and sex assigned at birth align) and transgender people like me (people whose gender identities and sex assigned at birth don't line up).

My story greatly impacted my school community. One of my

students immediately texted his mom that his favorite teacher, me, was transgender—just like his older brother! His mom later told me I had become a powerful role model for him in seeing his brother's transness differently: now he had an image of what a trans man could be like as a successful adult. This made me realize how vital it was for me to be out and visible—not just for the trans students I might teach, but also for the family members and friends of transgender people!

Being out and visible to my students as trans and queer inspired me to be out and visible at Math for America (MfA), the fellowship of math and science teachers that had sustained me during my entire teaching career. Although I was out to many of my MfA friends, I had not advocated for any changes within the organization. Instead, I had allowed my passing privilege to allow me to opt-out of that work. That spring, I asked why MfA didn't have a contingent in the Pride March—and received support to create the first group! The following fall, two queer colleagues asked me to co-facilitate a course on affirming our LGBTQ+ students in STEM, and this inspired me to create an LGBTQ+ affinity group for the MfA adults. We met regularly and discussed the challenges we faced—in our schools, classrooms, and even at MfA. We discussed the challenges of bathrooms and pronoun-shares, and two of us brought our concerns to the director of the program.

The seventeenth floor, where most of our MfA programming was held, had only two multi-stall bathrooms and no single-use stalls, creating an issue for non-binary members of our community. I proposed something radical. What if we had multi-stall, all-gender restrooms with signs indicating what facilities were inside each room rather than the gender of the people who "should" be using it? I referenced the bathrooms on my college campus and convinced the director that this was feasible. We decided to offer "gendered bathrooms" on the sixteenth floor. If someone needed gender-segregated bathrooms, they would have the option but would also experience having to go to another location. Usually, it is the non-binary and gender non-conforming people who need to travel to find an acceptable bathroom. With this plan, they would have a peaceful and normative bathroom experience.

Having gender neutral bathrooms available and visible to all community members can do a lot to create a welcoming space for trans and gender-non-conforming people. Knowing that it's a priority for my organization to make space for us and our needs makes me feel included. My college battle for bathrooms armed me with the evidence necessary to make a convincing argument. These experiences also helped me recognize the importance of being the supportive teacher I needed when I struggled with making sense of my own gender in middle school and high school.

KIT GOLAN is a Math for America Master Teacher in his tenth year of teaching math at a public middle school in New York City. He is dedicated to crafting experiences for his students that invite them to mathematize their lives and see math as a tool for making sense of, explaining, and evaluating their lives. Kit also serves as a co-advisor for his school's Gender and Sexuality Alliance and recently organized a contingent of his MfA fellowship teachers for the NYC Pride March. He constantly reflects on his teaching practice, both in writing and at storytelling events.

Social Action Activity for "Bathrooms for All"
Powering and growing your activism skills through identity work

At the beginning of this book, Val Brown asks us to consider the question: *How can my learning inform my strategy?*

The focus of this activity is to reflect, individually or in community, on how your identity and personal history, with all its facets, positively impacts your skillset and stance as you undertake social action. Think about how you can grow, using your identity and history as a strong foundation.

Kit's identity work helped him see why being out in professional spaces could be meaningful for himself, his students, and his colleagues. But Kit's identity of being trans isn't his only identity at play: he's a math teacher, and he's learned to leverage and encourage the same logical reasoning, based on evidence, in both his classroom and his advocacy.

Take some moments to reflect, in writing or a voice recording, on the following prompts:

What are **three aspects** of your (or your organization's) identity or history that are most important or most urgent to you right now? For each, describe briefly why this aspect matters to you.

Choose one of these aspects of identity or history. Write or speak about the strengths you hold that result from this aspect. (If you are new to identity work, or if the identity you're considering has negative connotations for you right now, you might need to seek out some mentor texts. How do other people of similar identity or history celebrate the experience or worldview you share? What do they see as strengths or positives?)

Repeat with the other two aspects of identity or history that you identified in the first step.

Review your thinking. Where do you see overlaps? Where do you see opportunities for growth and learning? How might you leverage the strengths of one or more of your identities in your activism work in new ways, or synergistically?

If you're doing this activity in community or in the context of an organization, come back together to share your insights as a team. What might you learn from one another? Where might you grow? How can your learning from this identity work inform your strategy?

FINDING IDENTITY IN COMMUNITY

ADELINA ARAGON IN CONVERSATION WITH REBECCA VAN TASSELL

Our identities are integrated with our communities. Sometimes, our work in community shapes our identity more than our identity shapes our community. For Adelina, her strong desire to create support for other mothers in her community became the support she needed.

REBECCA: BECOMING A MOTHER CAN BE A LONELY ENTERPRISE. A considerable change occurs in our identity, in our capacity to love, and in our bodies. Navigating these changes can leave you feeling isolated, alone, and unsure of yourself. But some mothers in Poughkeepsie, New York, have a place to go to not be alone.

Adelina Aragon is a multilingual mother of two, a peer educator for the Centering Pregnancy program at Hudson River Health Care, and an organizer for the Mother's Project. I met Adelina through my mother-in-law, Kay Bishop, the midwife who founded and coordinates the programs in which Adelina participates and leads. In the conversation from which this story is edited and condensed, Adelina told me how she became involved with these programs and what they mean for her and her community.

I am a White woman, and we wanted this story to be in Adelina's voice because it is her story to tell, not mine. The two of us spoke English, which is not Adelina's first language, because I do not speak Spanish. The following story is edited from the transcript of our conversation.

The Mother's Project: A support group for mothers

ADELINA: I felt so lonely after I had my first child. I was only at home; I didn't go anywhere. It was pretty much just go to doctors' visits and back home. And I felt sad that I didn't have time to go out. I was only at home, taking care of my husband, house, and child. During that time, I felt lost. I didn't work. It was hard. I felt I didn't have any purpose in life.

When I found out my son had autism, it was so emotional because I didn't have any information. The only thing I knew was severe autism. I didn't know there was a spectrum, and it was so hard. I was home alone with my son, thinking, crying, and I didn't know what to do. I had been to some meetings of the Mother's Group, and they were there to help me.

In the beginning, I felt like I didn't trust anybody. Like with the situation that I was going through with my son, I didn't talk about it at first, because I thought I was the only one. So, it was hard for me to open myself. But in this group, we talk about a lot of things that we are going through. Sometimes we have guest speakers, and sometimes we talk about mental illnesses. We built trust because everyone was opening something very little, day by day, opening a little bit about their stories. And that's how it made me feel safe.

The Mother's Project is a time for us to sit and chit chat about what we are going through in life and what we need. For example, regarding services, there's a mother who says, "I can't find a school because my child needs special education." And then another mother comes up and says,

"Oh, well, I'm going through the process as well" so we share information. And I feel it's becoming a family.

I get to bring my children and they get so excited. They think we are going to work: They're very happy and say, "Oh, we have to hurry up. We don't want to be late for work!" They get very, very happy—and I am so glad because they can come. And in a way, I can have my own time. And they can have their own time with the other kids who are like little brothers and sisters. Because my son has autism, he needs to talk and play with other kids where he feels safe.

I can have my own time with the other mothers, because I know they're going through a lot as well. They are working. They are students as well as mothers. Just to sit down at the table feels like such a relief. We're relaxing. We do a lot of projects, things that we don't sometimes get to do at home. Right now, we are working on a quilt. We come from different places, but here everyone has a piece, and we're drawing something personal, like something from our country. We are expressing something unique about ourselves in a piece of fabric, and we're starting to put everything together. It will make a big quilt, with a little piece from each one of us.. As we work, we get to share things. We talk about our days. It's like we're sitting at dinner, sharing openly. We are family.

Centering Pregnancy: Health care in community with others

REBECCA: Centering Pregnancy is a group prenatal care model. In this practice, women are seen as a group. Each person gets individual time with a midwife for taking vital signs and listening to baby's heartbeat, but the consultation portion of the visit is done in community with other women. Typically the group includes other women at the same point in their gestation, aligning the medical advice to be pertinent to all the women's stage of pregnancy. Adelina serves as a peer educator for the group and as a translator for the mothers.

ADELINA: I'm very happy for this new project we're working on because, when I was pregnant, I felt like there wasn't enough information for me. There were no groups for mothers, and I felt like we didn't have that support. Now that I'm working on this group—in some ways it is easy because I know a lot of the mothers and they know who I am. And the best thing is that I always treat them with respect. And that's how they feel: respected. I don't want them to feel lonely like I was. I try to make them feel special, that they worthy of the support.

As a peer educator, I take attendance, I give out flyers about the gestational age that they are in. And I asked them if they have any questions for the midwife. We can talk about anything: breastfeeding, how they are feeling at that time, or any issues or concerns that they might have. Some of them say, "Well, I can't sleep on this side, is it okay? Am I going to hurt the baby?" Or we discuss what to expect in labor: who can be there? What medicine is there? We can talk about anything. I translate everything.

They trust me and they are able to ask me questions that they might not ask the midwife. They're not afraid to say, "Okay, look, I'm going through this, or I need that—can you ask the midwife?" I feel that I'm the connection to the community. I was once in the situation that they're in now. When I was there, I needed a hand. Now I feel that I can be the person to help.

The best part is that I live here in this community. I'm here at the clinic and I represent them, so every time they see me here at the clinic, and when I see them outside, they say, "Oh, can I ask you a question?" and I say, "Yeah," and that's how it starts. "Okay, what do you do there?

Because I see you there." So, then I start to talk about what I do here, what projects that we have, what groups we have. And that's how they spread the word. They're shy sometimes. I don't know if it is that they are afraid to ask, but they are shy. It makes me feel great that they can trust me. And I can see the way they talk to me, the way they ask me questions, when they approach me with those questions. I live here, I am part of this community, they trust me.

More than just giving back

I'm so attached to this. Because I know this is the beginning. This is the beginning for us to become better every day. This is the support that we need now, so we can know how to be strong later on.

First, I was just a mom who used to come to the meetings. Then Kay (the midwife who organizes these programs) involved me in more of the planning for the Mother's Group, in addition to coming to share my experiences. Now I'm involved in the project where I can help. And that's how I realized I needed to start doing something else.

There was a time when I was in an abusive relationship. It was emotional. It was hard. He made me feel like I wasn't worth it. I went through things I never thought I was going to face. Coming to the mothers' group was affirming for me. The support I received allowed me to leave that relationship and start school.

I went to school. I registered. I went to a counselor and said, "I don't know what to study, but I want to be here." When I went to the career center, I started to talk about the Mother's Group. I told them everything that I did with the group.

And the counselor said, "You just don't know the name of it. It's human services, social work." I started to research what social work was.

And I was like, yeah, this is what I want to do. Hopefully, I'll be graduating in the fall, earning an Associate's degree in Human Services. I'm trying to get a bachelor's degree. I'm getting there little by little.

That's why I get up every day. Not just for my children, but myself, and for other moms who might be suffering from what I suffered. They probably don't know who or where to ask for help. Every day I come to the clinic; I have a smile for everyone. But at the end of the day, I just sit down on the couch with my children. Sometimes I cry because it has been challenging. My days are not easy, and it still is hard sometimes, even with everything I'm learning. Each day, I try to become better. If I'm okay, my children are okay.

I'm still learning that it's okay. It's okay to make mistakes. Sometimes we have to learn that we can't control everything, but the way we respond, what we do, that's what matters.

ADELINA AREGON is dedicated to the community and has managed to overcome many obstacles to achieve what she sets out to do. She believes that everything is possible, and that success comes from deep inside of yourself. Originally from Mexico, Adelina became a DACA student, facing a language barrier that did not stop her. This year, she graduated from Dutchess Community College with an Associate Degree in Human Services and is currently working for Family Services at the Children's Center as an intern and teacher. Adelina has been a health promoter and a peer educator for the Centering Pregnancy Program at Hudson River Health Care and has been part of the Mother's Project for ten years. She promotes the Guelaguetza cultural group as a folklore dancer, and she is also part of *"Hágase Contar* Census 2020" to educate the Latino community. She loves her family and is infinitely grateful to her partner, children, parents, and siblings for their support. Although she has worked hard and has earned many certificates, Adelina's most important and rewarding job is being a mother. Being an autism advocate for her son has made her more dedicated, hard-working, and strong.

Social Action Activity for "Finding Strength in Community"
Finding your identity through the work

In the previous activity, we asked you to find ways that your identity can power the work and learning you do. This activity asks a converse question: what can we learn about our identity, about who we are and who we are becoming, through reflecting on the work, people, and experiences that we have found meaningful, rewarding, or valuable?

Start by telling yourself or others a story of an activity, relationship, or event that's been a meaningful, positive experience for you. You can write in a journal, type in a digital document, speak in a voice recording, or sit in conversation with a trusted friend or family member.

After you tell the story, see if you can identify one or two values that the experience or relationship embodies for you. Examples of values include peace, resourcefulness, growth, and connection; a quick online search for a list of "personal values" or "core values" will provide you with many to consider. Once you've identified the personal values that matter to you from this experience, think about how those values exist in your life currently—or how you'd like them to exist. How can you find ways to center, redirect, or celebrate your identity through these values?

Again, this activity is equally powerful individually or in community.

I AM FROM NOT KNOWING WHEN HER CAR WILL COME THROUGH THE SNOW

Kirstin J. Milks

The actions and experiences of both teachers and students in American high schools are awash in issues of equity, diversity, access, and privilege that comprise both our nation's present and its history. In this piece inspired by George Ella Lyon's poem "Where I'm From," Kirstin asks us, regardless of profession or background, to examine our assumptions about where the people around us might be coming from. Student names used in this story are pseudonyms.

It's January the winter I am fourteen. I am standing outside my high school in upstate New York, watching flurries build to heavy snow in the orange glow of the parking lot.

To my left looms the solidity of the drama teacher. We are standing shoulder to shoulder, parka to parka, both gazing silently across the playing fields to where the school's long driveway meets Watervliet Shaker Road, almost a quarter mile away.

My house is one-point-one miles in the opposite direction.

The drama teacher and I are standing here because practice for the school musical ended an hour ago. Students—including me—streamed cheerfully from the auditorium to flood the hallway payphone with quarters and requests for rides.

When cars arrived and then departed, I waited. After all, she'd picked up the phone. She told me she was on her way.

Since then, I've spent my last two dollars on my family's answering machine. Even my long-standing "theater friend" from Dunsbach Ferry (miles up the road) is tucked into her home on the river by now.].

───

I have a lot of time to think here in the dark.

I think: She didn't sound great when she answered, lilting in a way that made me keep her on the line long enough to sing-song the plan back: Pick Kirstin up! Now! At the high school!

I also think: Where the heck is Papa?

I also think: I hope Julia's warm enough in the back seat. Wherever that is.

───

More than anything in this moment, what I want is for things in my life to be reliable.

Here is a partial list of what fourteen-year-old me considers reliable:

There is pretty much always food at this point.

The bus comes most days to take me to high school, where I am trying to win the heart of the kid who sits next to me in English class.

I get to read and write at school and think all day long without anything other than the occasional dodgeball being thrown at me. This level of physical safety contrasts somewhat with other situations in my life.

A partial list of the things fourteen-year-old-me considers unreliable:

My mother.

My father, who finds himself out late many nights now. For work.

And our bathtub, which I worry might sink even further and crash through the floor to the basement while I'm standing in the shower some morning.

═══════

Look, if I can't have reliability, please just let me have the slow, slippery, private walk home.

Please, one private walk back to the private uncertainty of my house.

But because I have already called home, I was told before the quarters ran out, we must wait—together, frozen.

═══════

I should just tell someone... Perhaps the drama teacher with the snow in his beard.

I am young, things are bad, my mother has not yet received an evaluation, and I find myself deciding to manifest the reliability I crave in my life. I'm going to do that, I discover, by explaining how this is a normal delay for a normal, attentive, reliable parent who lives a mile away from this school.].

"Happens all the time, her being this late," I suddenly say after forty-five minutes with a quick grin, a dismissive wave of my mittened hand that I hope will be particularly convincing.

And after that, I cannot stop my words from flooding out. I keep gesturing and talking about my average, reliable mom, taking care of us and our house and our dog and our cats, and starting to look for a teaching position.

The drama teacher murmurs politely.

For ten or so minutes.

And here's the thing: even as young and as hurt as much of me is at fourteen, I realize that this teacher here must smell trouble, that he must be able to hear beyond the words now pouring from me. But he doesn't stop me, so I keep on talking. Acting, an hour past drama practice.

And as it turns out, I *don't* stop. This first slippery telling of quarter-truths kicks off a decade-long compulsion to lie, again and again, about thousands of ordinary, everyday, unimportant things.

I can't stop the lies. I keep telling them. And those lies pile up like snow for that whole decade, burying me and freezing others out, until the person who is now my spouse looks me hard in the eyes and tells me I'm done.

———

So much of the memory I have from my adolescence is fogged, made incomplete by trauma.

But I can rewind the person that is me today—the person who's a high school teacher; a parent; a partner; you know, a *person*—back to this moment in a heartbeat, can suddenly find myself there and hear the hush of the snow around us, broken only by my small voice rising and falling.

And I can do this now because this moment is a significant inflection point for me.

It's a freeze-frame of truth that I then interpret disastrously for a decade.

And that truth, the truth I know in that moment, is that people don't necessarily want to hear the truth, because they don't know what to do with it.

I don't actually stand at the high school forever with the drama teacher, right? My mother must have come. Eventually, my kid sibling bundled into the back seat of the Buick.

The drama teacher is my classroom English teacher two years later. It's during the horrible year when my mother is removed from our home and doesn't return. By then, I'd quit the plays. Instead, I run the spotlights from high above the crowd, again shoulder to shoulder with the drama teacher.

We never, ever talk about the hour in the snow.

And I don't think I talk about it with anybody. Not with my sibling, not with the kid from English class whose heart I win. Not even with my mother, when we're finally able to talk.

Until it's fifteen years later, and I am a high school teacher myself, and I'm walking Clayton to the social worker, and Clayton is sobbing so hard he starts to gag in the hallway.

And it's three months after that when Lila's telling me a story about her family and I get this flash of insight that it might be just that—it might be a story, a set of falsehoods like the ones I told the drama teacher, and now I'm the teacher, and I need to decide what to do.

I find myself at school with Clayton and Lila and other kids, and I start telling tiny pieces of the story of this night in the snow, chipping off just enough of my story to draw out their stories.

And also, I realize, I want to show students an example of a time when things have ended up okay for someone they know, that we can grow out of and through the complicated stuff, especially when we get help.

I'm a high school science teacher; it's a job I anticipated to be about lab reports and nerdy puns. But it is an unexpected, enormous, and delightful part of my job to listen, carefully, to my emerging adults when they share stories about their lives. And it's my responsibility to help them use their stories to build their future selves, as learners and as people.

———

Now I don't blame the drama teacher, and I want to be clear about this with you.

I know from experience that this was one of the countless uncertainties and exhaustions that come with teaching. And, you know, maybe he did start a conversation with a guidance counselor, or call my father to check-in.

But now I wish, so much, that he had started that conversation with me, that he had checked in with me, there, in the snow.

I'm not saying I think all my shame about my family, all the fallout I've experienced from lack of proper parenting, our family's food insecurity, my own mental health, I'm not saying that all of that would have been fixed.

But it might have been a start.

———

For so many reasons, I am grateful to have found and married the person I am proud to call my spouse. But I am perhaps most grateful that he gave me a start, that he gave me the startle of not leaving, of telling me it was time to change and grow. He called me in, called to me from beyond my snowbank of unlovable falsehoods.

It's still not always easy. When I experience stress—despair, anger, or uncertainty—I still feel falsehoods icing up under my words and thoughts.

But Frank saw me, and he loved me enough to help me feel the traction, the power, of talking about the truth. He's helped me to explore my own true stories—including ones I am still learning to tell about experiencing childhood trauma. And these stories, my true stories, are part of how my students and I work together and how we talk together, and how I can be there for them.

For some of my students, it changes their lives. This year, I have been the first person that some students have talked to about the hunger they're facing, the abuse in their homes. I have been the person several students first tell about their desire and their plans to take their own lives. And I am so grateful every time a kid lets me help them get help. Every time.

———

Frank wisely warns there is a danger in me telling you this story. Because a teacher waking up and deciding "today I'm going to listen!"? It might not be enough. Being enough in this way as a teacher means you have to understand what stories might be out there in the world. Gain that understanding, and you can recognize the underlying stories of the people—in teachers' contexts, of the students—who come your way.

I think the best way to gain that understanding is to read and listen broadly. Seek out storytelling from all sorts of people who aren't like you, who don't live in places where you do. Otherwise, I think you risk what Chimamanda Ngozi Adichie describes as "the danger of a single story," cutting off possibilities in framing the world and the people in it for yourself and your students.

I think of what I'm learning through seeking out many voices as a collection of possibilities for my students' experiences. And this knowledge I've built, this map of probability space, is what makes me able to ask the next question, make the next move, to be a trustworthy adult without mining for students' trauma and creating more harm.

―――

This is why I want to start conversations with kids—both within the context of the content I teach and beyond—and I want to listen, *really listen* to what they have to say. And I want to be someone who fact-checks a kid as a way to say, "I see you. I notice you. I love you. And your situation is not impossible."

I want to be a person who *wants* to hear the truth, who knows the power of truth in helping create inflection points in our lives.

And I want my students, as grown-ups, to be open to exploring their own stories and to walk with others and *their* stories—as a start.

KIRSTIN J. MILKS learns from and with science students at Bloomington High School South in Bloomington, Indiana. She's committed to engaging students in authentic scientific and personal practices, collaborating with students and community members to create inclusive spaces and opportunities, and supporting and making public the work of teaching and learning. Kirstin is a National Board-Certified Teacher and a Senior Fellow at the Knowles Teacher Initiative, where she is editor-in-chief of the journal *Kaleidoscope: Educator Voices and Perspectives*.

―――

Social Action Activity for "I Am From Not Knowing When Her Car Will Come Through The Snow" Inflection Points

Lynda Barry's work in coaching storytellers and visual artists inspired this activity.

Privately select an inflection point in your own life, a moment when something changed for you or in your trajectory. It should be a moment that is important to you and your story. If you are doing this in community, however, you might consider picking something "in the middle"—not too shallow, but not so deep, dangerous, or painful that it will be overwhelming to live there for a few minutes.

Imagine yourself back at that inflection moment in your past and begin to write answers to questions like: Who is with you? When is this moment? Where? What are you hearing? Smelling? Tasting? Feeling on your skin or with your hands or feet? Look to your left; what do you see in this moment? What about right? Up? Down?

After this exercise in capturing descriptive detail, describe in writing how this moment served as an inflection point for you. Share with others—either about your writing directly or about your experience as you completed this writing—as appropriate.

By placing ourselves in a moment in our lives and reliving it with all our senses, we can begin to think more deeply about what it's meant and how it's affected us, allowing us the opportunity to build strength, courage, compassion, or insight as we chart our social action course.

AN EXCEPTIONAL MOM

CHRISTY MARIE KENT

*How do our identities change over time? How do those changing
perceptions and knowledge feed into our identities as social activists?
Christina reflects on both these questions, noting it wasn't until she lost
the privilege of being a White man that she realized there was so much to
protest for. Her story reminds us that, although we can't go back in time, we
can make choices right now that reflect our values.*

MOST MOMS ARE THERE FOR THEIR KIDS' FIRST DAY OF SCHOOL and first
report card. A really cool mom is there for her kid's first booze. But only
an exceptional mom is there for her kid's first protest march.

Understand that I didn't come from protest people. My dad was a
Southern Baptist minister, and not even the fire-and-brimstone kind. His
idea of raucous activism was standing up in church and praying, "Lord,
keep the homeless in thy hands. Let them find food and a warm place to
sleep."

Nevertheless, my twenty-one-year-old son and I march up Marquette
Avenue, joining seven thousand of our newest friends, chanting, "Families
belong together!" At each intersection, we turn to the waiting cars and

yell, "No more deportation camps!" We look directly at the TV cameras filming us from the skyways or the hundreds of people watching from sidewalks and parking ramps. We raise our fists in solidarity and shout, "Abolish ICE!"

Our crowd stretches for six city blocks. We march from the Minneapolis convention center to the Hennepin County Jail, along the way mopping the sweat from our foreheads on this sweltering summer day. At the courthouse, people gather around and listen to the guest speakers. Others find welcome seats on the grass by nearby buildings, where the shade provides almost-cool relief after tramping on hot asphalt. Meanwhile, the speakers shout their speeches into the PA system. Their words echo off the skyscrapers. It's fitting they're screaming about keeping families together right here, in front of the Hennepin County Jail, where so many families have been ripped apart.

Afterward, on our way back to the light rail, my son confides that part of the reason he's at this particular march is that he's met a Bangladeshi girl. She came here recently to live with her aunt and uncle, and he's thinking of asking her out. I don't know if she's here legally, and it doesn't matter because families belong together. This is one more reason I'm proud of him. And, I must admit, I'm also kind of proud of myself for being such an exceptional mom, taking her kid to his first protest march.

The train is packed, standing room only, shoulder to shoulder. I'm squished between my son and a lady holding her baby. After a few stops, the crowd thins enough so I can move up the aisle. There I hear a woman explaining she met her Peruvian husband at *Machu Picchu*. Her cute-as-a-button six-year-old daughter beams and says,

"Yeah, I'm half Latina!"

Her mother says, "We learned lots of new words today, didn't we, hon? We learned about detention centers and deportation." Words that a six-year-old half-Latina shouldn't have hear.

Finally, the seat next to me opens up. I'm about to sit when I notice the woman with her baby, still standing by the door. I wave her back to the seat. If anyone needs to sit, it's her. Then I noticed her pro-immigration shirt and asked if she came from the march. "Yeah, I didn't have a sitter today. But it's never too early to get him started in activism, is it?"

A few minutes ago, I was feeling exceptional for bringing my twenty-one-year-old son. Now, between the woman with her six-year-old half-Latina daughter and the one holding her nine-month-old baby, I'm not exceptional. I'm not even adequate!

She says, "It's not like that. Probably when yours were this young, there wasn't as much to protest."

"Yeah, that's it!" So nice that she gave me an out. "My kids were born in Nashville in the nineties, when the Cold War was over and 9/11 hadn't happened yet. The economy was booming, we had good jobs, and we bought a new home in the suburbs. The scariest thing in our lives was Barney the purple dinosaur."

"Weren't even more immigrants coming in back then?" she asks.

"Sure. California had a huge anti-immigration push."

"Did you protest that?"

"No. Mostly it didn't affect me. If anything, I benefited because immigrants took the jobs no one else wanted. You know how hot it gets laying asphalt shingles on a roof on a sweltering Tennessee summer afternoon? They couldn't find workers to do it, so the Hispanics came in and did those jobs."

"Or washing dishes."

"Or working in chicken processing plants. Hispanics filled those jobs, too. Americans need their McNuggets."

"What about the Defense of Marriage Act?" she asks. "Wasn't that passed in the nineties?"

"Oh, that's right!" I say. "I forgot DOMA. No one was even talking about gay marriage, much less protesting it. It wasn't a thing. Not till Republicans made it a wedge issue to fire up their base. It wasn't just DOMA, either. They passed one-man-one-woman laws and constitutional amendments across the country. I voted against it in Tennessee, but the conservatives won anyway."

"Did you protest it?" she asks.

"Well, no. My lesbian friend Nancy did."

Please don't ask why I didn't. I don't want her to ask because I don't have a good answer. I consistently voted to protect other people's rights, but when voting didn't work, I never screamed. Mostly because it didn't affect me, so I put my objections away until the next election.

She doesn't pry, of course, because she's a Minnesotan. She tosses me a softball question instead. "What made you become an activist?"

"That's easy. When it became personal."

In the 2000s, I came out as trans. That's when I learned what it meant to be discriminated against. After conservatives lost the war on same-sex marriage, craven politicians who needed someone to demonize shifted their focus to people like me. They introduced bathroom bills in statehouses across the country—including here in Minnesota—to stoke fear and hatred against *me*. They told their voters I only wanted to use the women's restroom so I could rape your daughters. They did this not because trans people are lesser citizens, not because we were doing anything illegal, but solely because they believed we were vulnerable.

Only when I lost my White male privilege, I finally learned how much privilege I started with—and how those with less privilege experienced life. My activism evolved, not only for trans people, but for other vulnerable groups, too. That's when I became a more active protester, mainly through my storytelling and writing. On the day after Trump's inauguration, I participated in the women's march in St. Paul. Now I'm at the immigration march.

"It was easy to become an activist when it became personal," I say. "But not ideal. I should have been out there fighting for everyone else. The truth is, we had just as much to protest back in the nineties. I just had some growing up to do first."

She says, "Well, you must have done something right back then, because your son's here protesting with you now."

"Yeah," he says, finally chiming in. "You raised me better than your parents raised you."

Which, really, is all any mother can hope for.

"If I had a do-over for the nineties," I say, "I'd protest everything. I'd fight the one-man-one-woman laws that kept good people from marrying the people they love. I'd protest the crime bill that locked nonviolent Black fathers in prison. I'd work to circumvent voter suppression laws and immigration restrictions. Unfortunately, I can't go back and change my behavior twenty-some years ago, but I can change what I do now."

"It's okay," my son says. "Even if it's too late to be an exceptional mom, you can still be the cool mom."

"Yeah?"

"Sure," he says. "On the way home, let's stop at the liquor store."

CHRISTINA MARIE KENT was born in Mississippi and lived all over the South. Her day job in insurance moved her further and further north until she found herself living in the frozen tundra of Minneapolis with her husband, two sons, and a cat that begs her to return to a warmer climate. She is a champion storyteller and writer. Her second novel, *Transgression*, came out in April 2019.

Social Action Activity for "An Exceptional Mom"
Looking behind, moving forward

We all have been in the position of inaction that Christy explores. Often, there are important reasons for our inaction. Analyzing those times may help us understand why we've chosen to act or not act and can help us choose action in the future. We also sometimes feel that our efforts have had no impact.

In both cases, sharing stories can illuminate the underlying reasons, values, and motivations for our action or inaction. This exploration can serve several purposes: it can allow us to know ourselves better, affirm our own experience when we listen to others' stories of struggle to act, and change how we align our values to action in the future.

For this exercise, think of a time when you chose inaction instead of action. What did you tell yourself about this choice? Were you too busy? Was the action intimidating? Whatever the reasons, explore the story you have told yourself about this time of inaction.

Share this story with another person, and hopefully, your partner will share a story with you. After you have shared, talk about your reasons for inaction. How do they feel now? Do your choices live out your values and ideals, or are they misaligned?

What could you change to better align your future choices with your values? What plan for action can you make, no matter how small?

EPILOGUE

WHEN WE SOLICITED STORYTELLERS FOR THIS BOOK and stories came pouring in, the first Covid-19 diagnosis was many months in the future. As we write this, with so much of our society disrupted and unsure because of Covid-19, one thing is for certain: we need the power of stories more than ever.

This is a time of difficulty, particularly for people mourning loved ones and for our society's most vulnerable—but also for all of us. We need stories in times of difficulties—stories of survival, stories of triumph, stories of laughter, and stories of heartache. Stories help us dream a better world into being by opening us to what's possible and how we might work towards it.

The three of us on the editorial team know that our contributors' experiences, knowledge, and actions are critically important. We know that reading and reflecting on these stories will help you explore your own experiences, knowledge, and actions. And we know because we've explored together as we've edited this book.

Through this work, we have learned just how much our identities and experiences shape our perspectives. We've explored our options when our team finds itself inadvertently giving priority to working structures rooted in our previous experience rather than our dreams of what could be possible. For us, naming a disconnect and encouraging open discourse about perspective often helped us see a way forward that allowed us to match our actions to our values, both individually and collectively.

We also found ourselves working to recalibrate our mindsets and actions around collaboration and community. For example, when we looked at early drafts of the language we'd generated to introduce and follow up on the stories in this book, we realized we'd fallen into positioning the contributors as superheroes. Our prose was filled with celebrations of "ordinary people doing extraordinary work" and adjectives touting the individuals telling the stories as exemplars, rather than examples.

Storytelling can serve, to paraphrase Dr. Rudine Sims Bishop's framework, as a mirror held up to ourselves and as a window into the lives and experiences of others. In this case, we used the mirror of our early drafts to overhaul our positioning and redefine our plans for including our storytellers in the editing and publishing process.

But we wouldn't have been able to see what we saw in the mirror of our prose without the work of others. For example, Cornelius Minor's work on decolonization in education helped us shift the power we held, as editors, into the hands of contributors. Learning for Justice's work on anti-bias frameworks helped us describe how identity was at play in our work, which in turn enabled us to make more equitable choices about how we represent our positioning and experiences. And this collection's magnificent stories themselves helped us see where we could make changes for the better, in ourselves and our work.

We hope you find strength and perspective through the stories in this volume. We hope our suggestions for activities help you learn more about yourself and others' unique perspectives and open windows for you to see a more hopeful future. And we hope you see that there are many others standing with you on the road to freedom and justice.

For the world and for ourselves, we must work to continue to tell and seek out stories of resilience, resistance, and resoluteness. We owe it to each other to find stories of social action in the narratives of our world, so people become visible, represented, and heard. Any story shared, even with just one person, is a step along the path to achieving equity in our communities and beyond. We hope to hear from you, our readers, and the storytellers we have yet to meet to hear these stories of change.

—Kevin, Kirstin, and Rebecca

CREDITS

"Dandelion" first appeared in *Diving in the Moon*, the Healing Story Alliance journal.

A version of "Storm-stayed" first appeared in *Pulse—Stories from the Heart of Medicine*.

A version of "Having Difficult Conversations" and an audio version of "I Am From Not Knowing … " first appeared in *Kaleidoscope: Educator Voices and Perspectives*.

A version of "Deep Dive" received the Pearl Buck Award from the West Virginia Writers Association.

"Cric? Crac!" is excerpted from the introduction to *Supporting Diversity and Inclusion with Story: Authentic Folktales and Discussion Guides*, edited by Lyn Ford and Sherry Norfolk (Libraries Unlimited, 2020).

ABOUT THE EDITORS

KEVIN D. CORDI, PH.D. (he/him), serves as an Assistant Professor at Ohio University Lancaster. For over twenty-five years, he has told stories as a professional storyteller in over forty states, England, Japan, Singapore, Scotland, and Qatar. According to the National Storytelling Network, he is the "first full-time high school storytelling teacher in the country." Kevin is the author of *Playing with Stories: Story Crafting for Writers, Teachers, and Other Imaginative Thinkers* (Parkhurst Brothers, 2014) and *You Don't Know Jack: A Storyteller Goes to School* (University of Mississippi Press, 2019). He currently serves on the National Advisory Board for Teaching Tolerance and teaches equity, education, storytelling, and literacy classes. Kevin also hosts Storyville, true stories of diversity and community told LIVE and out loud.

KIRSTIN J. MILKS (she/they), learns from and with science students at Bloomington High School South in Bloomington, Indiana. She's committed to engaging students in authentic scientific and personal practices, collaborating with students and community members to create inclusive spaces and opportunities, and supporting and making public the work of teaching and learning. Kirstin is a National Board Certified Teacher and a Senior Fellow at the Knowles Teacher Initiative, where she is editor-in-chief of the journal *Kaleidoscope: Educator Voices and Perspectives*. She holds a Ph.D. in biochemistry from Stanford.

REBECCA VAN TASSELL (she/her), is an educator based in Bradford, Pennsylvania, whose experience includes teaching at a Midwestern comprehensive high school, an urban charter school, a wealthy suburban district, and the post-secondary level. Students have unique challenges navigating their way through adolescence in all these contexts, and Rebecca is committed to making schools humane places for students and teachers to learn together. Rebecca is a Senior Fellow at the Knowles Teacher Initiative, where she leads a writing workshop for secondary teachers and serves as editor-in-chief of the journal *Kaleidoscope: Educator Voices and Perspectives*. She believes in the power of storytelling to elevate teachers as knowledge generators in education.

If you have enjoyed this book, point your browser to:

www.parkhurstbrothers.com